UNDERSTANDING TUPE

Spiro Business Guides
Human Resources and Training

Spiro Business Guides are designed to provide managers with practical, down-to-earth information, and they are written by leading authors in their respective fields. If you would like to receive a full listing of current and forthcoming titles, please visit www.spiropress.com or email spiropress@capita-ld.co.uk or call us on +44 (0)870 400 1000.

New authors: we are always pleased to receive ideas for new titles; if you would like to write a Spiro Business Guide, please contact Dr Glyn Jones at spiropress@capita-ld.co.uk or call direct on +44 (0)1865 884447.

Bulk orders: some organisations buy a number of copies of our books. If you are interested in doing this, we would be pleased to discuss a discount. Please contact the Customer Centre on +44 (0)870 400 1000 or email spiropress@capita-ld.co.uk.

Understanding TUPE

A Legal Guide

Stephen Hardy

First published in 2002 by
Spiro Press
17–19 Rochester Row
London
SW1P 1LA
Telephone: +44 (0)870 400 1000

ISBN 1 904298 35 4

Reprinted September 2002
Ref 6044.JC.9.2002

British Library Cataloguing-in-Publication Data.
A catalogue record for this book is available from the British Library.

Disclaimer: This publication is intended to assist you in identifying issues which
you should know about and about which you may need to seek specific advice. It
is not intended to be an exhaustive statement of the law or a substitute for seeking
specific advice.

Spiro Press USA
3 Front Street, Suite 331
PO Box 338
Rollinsford NH 03869
USA

Typeset by: Monolith – www.monolith.uk.com
Printed in Great Britain by: Biddles, UK
Cover design by: REAL451

To Louise and Dominic with much love today and always

Contents

Preface and acknowledgements

Business transfers have increasingly become a prominent feature of labour law, employment relations and HR practice, as well as both European and British political dialogue over the last three decades since their legal advent. During that period, while their importance has grown, their legal clarity has diminished. This book hopes to remove the confusion surrounding this pertinent legal area and provide a clear pathway of understanding for those involved in business transfers.

First and foremost, my thanks go to Professors Richard Painter and Nick Adnett whose excellent doctoral supervision led to my fascination with the subject-matter being discussed. In addition, I owe thanks to the numerous officials of unions, employers' associations and government, especially the DTI. I also owe thanks to my JSB (Consulting and Training) colleagues and 'TUPE course' attendees whose views on TUPE have indirectly benefited this book in many ways. Lastly, Louise's love and patience has allowed this project to both exist and be completed as ever, even after the arrival of Dominic in mid-November 2000.

The law is stated as at 1 June 2001.

SH

Manchester 2001

Table of cases

Table of statutes

List of abbreviations

ACAS	Arbitration, Conciliation and Advisory Service
ARD	Acquired Rights Directive
CA	Court of Appeal
CBI	Confederation of British Industry
CCT	Compulsory Competitive Tendering
CEEP	Centre Européen des Entreprises à Participation Publique
CEPR	Centre for Economic Performance
CIPFA	Chartered Institute of Public Finance and Accountancy
CRE	Commission for Racial Equality
DE	Department of Employment (since 1995 Department for Education and Employment)
DLO	Direct Labour Organisation
DoE	Department of the Environment (DETR 1997–2001)
DRC	Disability Rights Commission
DSO	Direct Service Organisation
DTI	Department of Trade and Industry
EAT	Employment Appeal Tribunal

EC	European Community (1986–1992)
ECA	European Communities Act 1972
ECJ	European Court of Justice
ECSC	European Coal and Steel Community
EEC	European Economic Community (1957–1986)
EFTA	European Free Trade Association
ELA	Employment Law Association (UK)
EOC	Equal Opportunities Commission
EP	European Parliament
EPCA	Employment Protection Consolidation Act 1978
ERA	Employment Rights Act 1996
ERelA	Employment Relations Act 1999
ESC	Economic and Social Committee of the EU
ET	Employment Tribunal (1996–)
ETO	'Economic, Technical and Organisational' Defences (Regulation 8, TUPE 1981)
ETUC	European Trades Union Confederation
EU	European Union (1992–)
EWC	European Works Council
GMB	General Municipal and Boilermakers Union
HL	House of Lords
HMSO	Her Majesty's Stationery Office
HMYCC	Her Majesty's Youth Custody Centre
HRM	Human Resources Management
HSE	Health and Safety Executive
IER	Institute of Employment Rights

ILO	International Labour Organisation
INGLOV	Institute of Local Government
IRLR	Industrial Relations Law Reports
IT	Industrial Tribunal (1964–96)
LGIU	Local Government Information Unit
LGMB	Local Government Management Board
MEP	Member of the European Parliament
MP	Member of Parliament
NASUWT	National Association of Schoolmasters and Union of Women Teachers
NATFHE	National Association of Teachers in Further and Higher Education
NUCPS	National Union of Civil and Public Servants
OJ	*Official Journal* (publication of the European Union)
RCN	Royal College of Nursing
SAP	Social Action Programme
SoCPO	Society of Chief Personnel Officers (local government)
SOSR	'Some Other Substantial Reason'
SSP	Statutory Sick Pay
TEU	Treaty on European Union (Maastricht and Amsterdam Treaties)
TGWU	Transport and General Workers Union
TUC	Trades Union Congress
TULRCA	Trade Union and Labour Relations Act 1992
TUPE	Transfer of Undertakings (Protection of Employment) Regulations 1981

TURERA   Trade Union Reform and Employment
         Rights Act 1993
UK   United Kingdom
UNICE   Unions des Confédérations de l'Industrie et des
         Employeurs d'Europe
UNISON   The Public Sector and Health Union

About the author

Stephen Hardy JP, LLB, PhD, FRSA, ILTM is Senior Lecturer in Law at Manchester University, where he lectures and researches in EU, labour and company law. He obtained a PhD on business transfers and has since researched and published extensively on this subject. Consequently, he has become a recognised national authority on TUPE and its legal implications (the author is referred to as the 'TUPE anorak'), and has advised the government on TUPE issues. He lectures for the Chartered Institute of Personnel Development (CIPD) on business transfers and other employment law matters and acts as a tutor on the CIPD's Advanced Certificate in Employment Law Programme. He is also a Senior Consultant with JSB Consulting & Training, advising companies on EU and employment law matters, as well as conducting in-house training. Previously he has been a Visiting Lecturer at Dortmund (Germany), Paris (France) and Leicester (UK) universities. Dr Hardy has also worked at Staffordshire, Salford and UMIST (Manchester School of Management) universities, as well as for the EU Commission as a researcher in the European Parliament, and as an intern in the US Senate. He is currently researching into alternative dispute resolution in employment law, human rights at work and EU comparative employment law regulation. More recently, the author has been involved with assisting the States of Jersey government in drafting employment laws on trade union governance.

The author may be contacted via the publishers.

CHAPTER 1

Introduction and the origins of business transfers

Business transfers have increasingly become a commonplace occurrence across the European Union (EU) since the 1980s. As a result, their importance in employment law and HR practice has become paramount, since for employers 'business transfers' can either mean commercial survival or a symbol of success whereas employees' concerns focus on job security and terms and conditions. In this book a consideration of the inherent conflict of interest between business interests and contractual rights will be given. Notably, the widespread reorganisation of businesses and the extensive application of contracting-out in the UK's public sector since the 1980s has caused controversy between the employer's business interests and the employee's contractual rights has intensified. It is this conflict that this book aims to analyse while simplifying the law relating to business transfers in the UK in order that we may understand the relevant legal principles and identify good HR practice in this area.

The legal framework governing business transfers, its origins and its effectiveness is examined in this and Chapter 2, while Chapter 3 presents the HR context to business transfers. Chapter 4 explains the significance to business transfers of contracting-out and Chapter 5 discusses consultation and information issues. Chapter 6 gives current case law and some HR solutions to handling business transfers. The closing two chapters provide an analysis of the issues surrounding the new 1998 Amended Directive and the implications for the revised TUPE Regulations 2001. By way of conclusion, some useful HR checklists are provided and a legal strategy is developed. Overall, this book aims to help busy lawyers, other legal advisors and HR/business managers to make sense of this complex area against a background of rapidly changing case law and legislation. This opening chapter seeks to provide the necessary background and knowledge to embark upon this analytical journey through the myriad of legal, political, economic and HR issues that dominate the law surrounding business transfers.

Our starting point: the case of Mrs Dines

The cases of Mrs Dines, Sophie Bartol, Nicholas Betts, Albert Merckx, Anne Rask, Christel Schmidt, Ayse Suzen, Tony Wren, Oy Likenne and many others to be discussed in this book highlight some of the consequences of the current law relating to business transfers. Above all, the UK case of Mrs Dines, a hospital cleaner, demonstrated how UK business transfers operated under contracting-out can often result in a change in terms and conditions of employment. Faced with redundancy from her old employer, Basildon and Thurrock NHS Trust, Mrs Dines took up re-employment with the new contractor on less pay. Meanwhile, she also had the courage to complain to an Industrial (now Employment) Tribunal about the consequences of her business transfer undertaken in January 1991.

The Employment Tribunal (ET) concluded that even when companies enter into competition under contracting-out (such as compulsory competitive tendering (CCT) in her case), the fact that the successful company continues to employ the same workers and in the same place does not give rise to a business transfer protected under the Transfer of Undertakings (Protection of Employment) Regulations 1981 (TUPE). It is these Regulations that then implemented the 1977 original ARD (77/187, *OJ* 1977 L61/26) into English law and apply where there is a change of employer, providing for the automatic transfer of contracts of employment, collective agreements and trade union recognition. According to the ET in Mrs Dines' case, contracting-out was curiously exempt from these Regulations. The Employment Appeal Tribunal (EAT) (EAT/126/93, (1993) IRLR 521) supported contracting-out's exemption in its dismissal of Mrs Dines' appeal. Upholding the ET's decision, the EAT found that there was no business transfer, notwithstanding the guidance from the European Court of Justice (ECJ) on determining whether there had been a 'relevant' business transfer or not. The EAT's decision in the Dines case was most perplexing, since it is clear from the facts that had the EAT correctly applied the ECJ's criteria it would have upheld Mrs Dines' appeal. It appears that the ET had misdirected itself and the EAT could be accused of adopting the same erroneous reasoning.

On appeal, the judges attempted to clarify the law. Adopting the ECJ's 'purposive' approach towards the ARD, the Court of Appeal ((1994) IRLR 366) held that a business transfer had occurred since the service had retained its identity following the transfer. Accordingly, contracting-out fell within the scope of the ARD. Mrs Dines' victory supported the philosophy behind the ARD that employees' rights should be safeguarded when they become subjected to business transfers. Of importance to readers in the context of HR practice is the fact that Mrs Dines' case exposed a fundamental clash of philosophies between domestic and EU laws with regard to the regulation of business transfers. The *Dines* ruling marks our starting point as it clearly illustrates the legal conflict which exists on business transfers.

The importance of business transfers

Those involved with employment law or HR will have heard of TUPE. Before TUPE came into force in 1982 in the UK, the established common law (see *Nokes* v. *Doncaster Associated Collieries Ltd* (1940)) provided that, in the event of a business transfer, the existing contracts, being personal in nature, were automatically terminated and the employee became redundant. TUPE changed this long-standing legal position based on the freedom of contract, replacing it with a law which complied with EC Directive (77/187) – the Acquired Rights Directive (ARD). This Directive was passed to 'safeguard employees' interests in the event that a business in which they work was sold'. The Directive was motivated by a Report by the EU identifying the growth of business transfers in the

1970s. In 1990 another Report by the EU Commission (EU Commission's XXth Report on Competition Policy) showed that business transfers, during the 1980s, had doubled every three years at the EU level, accounting for 40% of the global number of business transfers. This puts the significance of business transfers into its rightful EU context. The law relating to transfers of undertakings, or business transfers as they are more commonly known, has since its advent been a peculiar feature of both English and European Community (termed 'Community') law, as it ties so many different legal strands together, such as company, commercial, insolvency and employment law, as well as 'new' questions about the development of EU social policy. With hindsight, the law relating to business transfers, due to its multifaceted nature, can almost be seen as a time bomb, ticking away since 1977, waiting to explode.

Business transfers can take place for several reasons. What is common about business transfers, unlike share transfers, is that they bring about a change in employer. The most common form of business reorganisation in the UK is by the transfer of share capital. These share transfers, as they are known, involve shares in a company becoming the property of another company. In share transfers, the identity of the employer remains the same and due to that fact in the UK they are distinct from legally protected business transfers, and as a result no legal protection is afforded to employees' terms and conditions. These business transfers are usually termed 'takeovers', 'mergers' or 'amalgamations'. Although Community law excludes share transfers from the ARD, some EU Member States have chosen to include them while others exclude them. In contrast, business transfers involving the sale or disposition of assets that do result in changes in the identity of the employer are legally regulated by the ARD. This distinction and its effects will be discussed further in the following chapter.

The evolution of UK employment law has since the 1940s demonstrated much legal flexibility towards business transfers, a position which was aptly described in the Nokes case (1940) by Lord Atkin as: '...the remarkable legal consequences of the courts [bringing] about this revolution in the law that led to companies being able to shake off the restrictions, only when they are minded to transfer their business to another and probably a larger company'. The importance of the contractual employment relationship, upon which UK employment law is founded, has therefore determined much of the course of British regulation, including the law relating to business transfers.

A historical context to transfers: social Europe versus UK policy

From 1974 to 1978, the 'Social Contract' period emerged in the UK influenced by the Donovan Report of 1968, which initiated an overall movement towards the creation of an 'industrial democracy'. This led in the 1970s to the development of a statutory framework of worker protection enacted under the Employment Act 1975 and the subsequent Employment Protection Consolidation Act 1978 (EPCA). It was also during the 1970s that the effect of the UK's membership of the EEC, now the EU, on domestic employment regulation was becoming apparent. This membership resulted in, among other obligations, the UK's acceptance of the ARD in 1977, although it was not fully implemented until 1982, the delay being caused by a change to a government opposed to the law brought about by the General Election of 1979.

With the new government in power throughout the 1980s in the UK policies were introduced based upon the supremacy of 'market forces' displacing employment law, as evidenced by an era of incremental deregulation. The UK's experiences of industrial strife in the 1970s gave much ideological impetus to the Thatcher administrations' deregulatory policies in the employment arena. With hindsight, it was becoming apparent that since the 1970s the seeds had been sown for the 'deregulation versus intervention' debate as seen in the 1990s.

Throughout the 1990s, the opposing camps of deregulation, depicted by a pervasive growth of individualism in the UK workplace, and intervention influenced by an ever-pervasive EU regulatory framework continued to be in conflict. Despite the UK's policies since 1979, the EU institutions continued to enforce the UK's obligations under the EU's 1957 Treaty of Rome. For example, from the 1980s it was emerging that while collective bargaining was being dismantled, EU membership was reconstructing employee protection, particularly in terms of equal treatment, anti-discrimination, collective consultation rights and business transfers. Consequently the UK government found its domestic employment policies being neutralised, if not undermined, by the efforts of the EU legislators. The law relating to business transfers significantly epitomised one point of the struggle within an overall policy for employment relationships and one which was important to the UK government's plan of resistance. This is significant because, as one of the first pieces of EU social legislation, it shows that the British position since 1979 has often been to reject EU efforts in that field.

The policy struggle between the UK and EU, reflected in the law relating to business transfers, heightened in the 1980s with deregulatory policies opposed to EU regulation. This resistance was maintained by the further dilution of employment protection rights releasing competitive forces in the labour market, as enacted in the UK by the Employment Acts of 1982, 1988, 1989 and 1990, the Trade Union and Labour Relations Consolidation Act 1992 (TULRCA), the Trade Union Reform and Employment Rights Act 1993 (TURERA) and the Employment Rights (ERA) and Industrial Tribunals (ITA) Acts of 1996.

In contrast, EU regulation continued to enhance worker protection under the banner of equal treatment (76/207). In the UK, the Equal Opportunities Commission (EOC) sponsored case, *R. v. Secretary of State for Employment, ex parte EOC* (1994) provides a useful illustration of the extensive application of EU laws to enforce change in domestic laws and workers' rights (now seen in the Part-Time Workers Regulations 2000). The fact that the UK government had persistently until 1997 opted out of EU social policy clearly demonstrated that two different philosophies were underpinning EU and UK employment, including business transfers.

A catalogue of cases, both at EU and UK levels, to be discussed in detail in Chapters 2 and 6, show the extent to which these conflicting foundations of employment law clash and they also expose the weaknesses in the current law. In fact, in a UK context, most of the current debate has centred upon business transfers initiated under the UK government's contracting-out policy. The extensiveness of the litigation in the UK has provoked a heated debate which has not been extinguished by the amendments made by TURERA 1993, now re-enacted in s. 218 of the Employment Rights Act 1996. The UK government's contracting-out policy, further reconstituted in recent years as 'Best Value' has generated a self-induced problem incurring a morass of complexity which causes uncertainty for employers and employees alike.

During the mid-1980s, it became increasingly apparent to the UK government that the EU was the main countervailing force, in terms of social legislation. In fact, two ideologies were prevailing. One of the first creative pieces of EU legislation to be implemented which highlighted the alarming division between UK domestic employment law and EU labour law was the ARD. This was the product of the Social Action Programme adopted by the EU Council of Ministers in 1974, whose primary objective was to enforce the recognition of employees' rights, particularly when changes of ownership and employer took place. Even the Labour government of 1977 in the UK was not fully enthusiastic about the ARD, as evidenced by its amendment and weakening of the draft ARD proposed in 1974. These amendments were produced because of British fears about the Directive's repeal of the UK common law established in 1940. Furthermore, the UK Trades Union Congress (TUC) in 1978 preferred the pre-existing voluntarist approach and rejected the idea of works councils to enable consultation about prospective business transfers, mooted in the original draft ARD. The ARD was therefore not implemented in the UK until 1982, when the incoming Conservative government was forced to give effect to the ARD due to the EU Commission's threat to initiate infraction proceedings. Such action clearly demonstrated the pervasive nature of 'social Europe'.

The pervasive nature of Community law

The UK has been a signatory to the 1957 Treaty of Rome and a Member State of the EU since 1 January 1973. As noted above EU membership has had a profound affect on the UK's constitutional framework, our legal system and, in particular, UK employment laws and practice. Of most importance is the fact that, as a consequence of EU membership, EC (Community) law prevails over UK domestic law where incompatibilities arise and the UK is bound by the Treaty provisions and the rulings of the ECJ, as prescribed by s. 2(1) of the European Communities Act (ECA) 1972. Consequently, Community law is not something that stands separate from domestic law; it is part of it, and enforceable as much before the British courts and tribunals as the European Court of Justice in Luxembourg. Due to the UK's EU membership, British employment law and HR practice is subjected to the protective labour standards of some EU partners and emanating from the EU, as seen for example in the standards relating to equal pay and treatment, free movement of workers and business transfers.

The EU Commission's 'Social Action Plan' of 1989 (COM (89) 568) marked pivotal progress towards developing a 'Social Europe', built upon a belief that providing a common European standard in economic, social and monetary activities would bring about closer integration, an aim set in 'The Preamble' of the 1957 Treaty of Rome. However, it was not until 1991, when the Maastricht Treaty

– the so-called Treaty on European Union (TEU) – was concluded that the social aspect re-emerged. The EU Social Action Programme for 2001 contains five key themes: employment; the development of legislation; equality of opportunities; an active social dimension; and a developing and ongoing social action plan. Within this Social Action Programme lay key proposals to tackle job growth and control widespread European unemployment, to commence education and training schemes and to maintain a high level of free movement, so as to create a fully integrated European labour market. Of central importance is the declaration contained in the Social Action Programme to 'encourage high labour standards as part of a competitive Europe', as well as a stronger commitment towards 'a more effective application of European law', which was expanded upon at the 1998 Amsterdam Summit and the resultant revised Treaty (especially Article 137). Such a programme places business transfers at its centre, given that it encapsulates all its aims.

What are 'business transfers' – the central terms

The term of art 'business transfer', or 'transfer of undertaking' as it is legally known, does much to confuse the labour lawyer, employer and employee because it is surrounded by a morass of legal complexities. At its simplest level, a business transfer connotes a change of ownership of 'any trade or business', either commercial or non-commercial, within the UK.

The original 1977 ARD, as transposed into English law by the TUPE Regulations 1981, provided for the pre-existing contracts of employment and terms and conditions, with the exception of occupational pensions, to be transferred to the new employer.

After a business transfer has taken place, identifying the employer is the most important question to all concerned. It involves not searching for an individual, but a legal entity: that entity being either a partnership, company or statutory body. It is here that the principle of freedom of contract allows for the employer's identity to be determined between the parties themselves. In other words, the concept of a 'transfer of an undertaking', albeit mechanical, does require some negotiation and consultation between the contractual parties. Business transfers, therefore, are technical legal instruments, as they concern the mobility of a 'going concern'.

Other key terms are :

- *transferor* – old/former employer, seller/vendor of the business;

- *transferee* – new employer, buyer/purchaser of the business;

- *transfer* –the change of ownership of a business (the legal defintion will be considered in Chapter 2).

'Shares' and 'assets' business transfers

In 1977, the EU Commission wanted to reduce some of the complexity by including share transfers within the ambit of the ARD (*OJ* C104, September 1974). During the course of the negotiation of the ARD among the EU Member States, its scope was narrowed and the EU Commission's desired proposal was deleted from the text. It is this historic deletion that has left a controversial legacy for the current UK law relating to business transfers. The overwhelming political pressure from EU Member States which resulted in the exclusion of share transfers in 1977 has caused much of the complexity surrounding the term of art a 'transfer of undertaking', ordinarily referred to as a 'business transfer'. This exclusion was confirmed in the *Brooker* v. *Borough Care Services* (1998) where it was held that there will be no transfer in accordance with TUPE where there is merely a sale of shares, since the legal identity of the employer remains the same.

Some EU Member States, such as France, for instance, chose to include share transfers when transposing the ARD into domestic law. In an EU context, both the Third and Sixth Council Directives (78/855, *OJ* L295 and 82/981, *OJ* L378 – see also ss. 425–7, Companies Act 1985 and the Companies (Mergers and Divisions) Regulations 1987) concerning public limited liability companies state that the ARD applies to mergers and divisions. Mergers, as defined under the Third Council Directive, refer to situations where one or more companies are transferred to another company by share acquisition. Normally, the members of the acquired company or companies receive shares in the other joined company or companies, with or without an additional cash payment. As a result, following the transfer of the assets and other liabilities, the acquired company or companies cease, as a general rule, to exist.

Despite attempts to include protection for employees subjected to share transfers (for example, see the Takeovers and Mergers (Employee Protection) Bill 1987) these 'atypical transfers' such as company takeovers by share purchase are not statutorily regulated at this time. These transfers are excluded because there is no change of employer. A takeover by means of share transfer is also clearly excluded from protection under the ARD, as recently reaffirmed by the European Court of Justice (ECJ) in the 'Perrier' case (1995, IRLR 381 ECJ). What the EU Commission chose to do, and remains committed to, is to distinguish between sales of businesses externally by changes in the ownership of assets from the movement of shares internally. Examples of the latter include changes in the composition of a partnership of a company and takeovers of company share capital. This disparity of legal treatment between shares and assets transfers seems hard to justify when employees, either by way of share acquisition or the sale of assets, change employer. Regardless, the law has chosen to do so both at common law and under statute. However, under s. 38 of the 1999 Employment Relations Act the Secretary of State may make Regulations in relation to the treatment of employees subject to transfer in circumstances where no transfer exists or where TUPE disapplies, so as to make TUPE apply in any event.

The origins of the ARD

By 1972, there was an emerging view among the heads of government of the Member States that the EU (then EC) should adopt a policy of more rigorous action in the social field. This led to the Social Action Programme which was adopted by the Council of Ministers in 1974. The Social Action Programme produced a series of Directives which were adopted between 1974 and 1979 and which constitute the main body of Community labour law. Among these was the Acquired Rights Directive which was adopted in 1977. Unlike much of the development of UK employment law the origins of the ARD are not derived from the Donovan Commission (1968) but are European. In order to consider the origins of the ARD, our starting place is the Treaty of Rome that brought about the so-called enthronement of European Law.

EU law-making since 1975 has been fundamental in shaping the terms of both individual and collective labour law rights in the UK. As a consequence of this EU regulation, a number of major labour law controversies, particularly relating to the EU's desire to create a 'Social Europe' has led to the UK adopting an aggressive, anti-European stance when it comes to EU labour law. Closely associated with this EU–UK dispute about the sovereignty of labour law is the law relating to business transfers, established by the fact that the ARD was one of the first pieces of EU labour law that the UK was forced to adopt, having been pursued in infraction proceedings by the EU Commission, the provisions of which were belatedly transposed 'with a lack of enthusiasm' into UK law under the 1981 TUPE Regulations. The ARD, therefore, plays a salient role, both historically and contemporarily, in the debate surrounding the potential development of EU social policy and in explaining the current state of both the EC and UK law governing business transfers. However, in a UK context, the answer to the question 'why did we need the ARD?' lies behind the shortcomings of the common law, as highlighted by the House of Lords' decision in 1940 in *Nokes* v. *Doncaster Amalgamated Collieries Ltd.*

The common law underlying a contract of employment did not provide for any continuity of employment alongside any changes in ownership of a business. The House of Lords held that where a change in the legal corporate personality takes place, normally by the sale of assets, employees' contracts are terminated. The rule in Nokes was explicable on the basis of freedom of contract. Subsequently, protective statutory provisions were enacted in order to establish extra-contractual measures to allow for continuity under s. 218 of ERA 1996 (formerly Sched. 13, para. 17, EPCA 1978), s. 141 of ERA 1996 modifying both the common law and s. 94 of the 1978 Act by offering protection to the former employer by prohibiting the right of an employee to claim redundancy if, on the transfer, the employee refuses an offer of suitable alternative employment with the new employer. This resulted in immobilising employees from complaining about business transfers.

Other legal cases, such as *Lloyd* v. *Brassey* (1969), *Woodhouse* v. *Peter Brotherhood Ltd* (1972), *Pambakian* v. *Brentford Nylons Ltd* (1978) and *Melon* v. *Hector Powe Ltd* (1981), prior to TUPE had recognised the inherent weaknesses of the common law relating to transfers and so TUPE was much welcomed. The ARD reflects the more intensely regulative traditions of the mainland EU Member States' systems of labour law, despite no formal EU model on transfers being in existence prior to the ARD. As a result, the notion of the ARD was created purely by the EU Commission's panel of experts convened to draft a proposed Directive on business transfers in 1974.

Why 1977?

In the UK during the 1970s, statutory employee protection and collective bargaining was promoted. This was an ideology which was challenged during the 1980s and 1990s in the UK by a government seeking to replace statutory labour protection with the notion of individualism in the workplace. In contrast, for the EU the 1970s marked an era of social policy-making, with the EU's institutions actively legislating under a common aim to initiate social legislation so as to bring about a closer integration in Europe. This was clearly demonstrated by its proposed Social Action Programme of 1974, which planned to facilitate social policy within the EU (then the EC) in order to counterbalance the existing emphasis upon economic activities. When the 1974–76 Social Action Programme was being conceived, the EU had to be seen to be more than a device to enable capitalists to exploit the common market; otherwise it might not be possible to persuade the peoples of the Community to continue to accept the discipline of the market. It was this Programme that marked the beginning of the recognition of the limitations of a simple adherence to economic theory underlying the liberalisation of trade and market enlargement for the free flow of goods and the advancement of social aims.

By 1974, the EU Commission, in light of the differences in unit labour costs throughout the EU and the higher profile of the free movement of both goods and workers, sought to institute some control over business transfers. The end result of these concerns was the 1977 ARD, albeit a watered-down version of the many earlier drafts produced by the committee of experts. The ARD was one of three directives born out of the 1974–76 Social Action Programme, which also created directives to encourage greater worker representation and provide social protection. The EU Commission also recognised a need to protect workers from the economic activities affected under the EU's Treaty provisions. The Treaty's provisions highlighted a deficiency, in terms of worker protection, when business transfers among Member States take place. Business transfers had to be regulated in order to bring the provisions for consultation in line with those pre-existing rights already in the Collective Redundancies Directive 1976 (75/129).

In 1977, it was becoming very clear that the role and use of employment law in the UK was changing due to the harmonisation of labour laws throughout the EU which was rapidly taking place. Although this EU social policy-making was motivated by economic factors, due to fears of competition distortion, particularly in terms of labour costs, it was an era in which the equal pay (75/117), business transfers and the collective dismissal directives established the first phase of EU social policy and social integration. During the 1970s, the ECJ's judicial activism was increasing due to its growing caseload and the ECJ was becoming a significant legislator in EU labour and social law.

The ARD was therefore a product of the EU Commission's discovery under Articles 118–122 (now Articles 134–141) of the Treaty that it had social policy aims founded by the Treaty of Rome. These social policy aims were to be pursued more actively throughout the 1980s, as evidenced by both the Single European Act 1986 and the 1989 Community Charter of the Fundamental Social Rights of Workers (the latter being revised and ratified at the Nice Summit, December 2000). The social provisions would allow a so-called 'harnessing of social policy' which would diminish the overall market-dominated approach of the Treaty. The ARD, therefore, contributed to the EU's march towards the notion of a 'Social Europe'.

Economics, politics and law interact with regard to business transfers. A salient point emerges out of such interaction: recessionary economic times create less interest in social protection. In the UK from the mid-1970s to the mid-1980s, the UK labour market saw widespread industrial action and the beginning of its fragmentation. In particular, from the 1980s, UK government economic policy began to dictate the displacement of some full-time workers with more commercially attractive, cheaper part-time labour. A so-called 'casualisation' of the workforce occurred. This pattern in the labour market became a hallmark of both Conservative economic and employment strategy throughout the 1980s.

The transposition of the ARD into TUPE in the UK Parliament

In 1981, the UK Parliament convened the political debate introducing the TUPE Regulations which transposed the controversial ARD into English law (for the House of Lords debate see Hansard HL 10.12.1981, col. 1490; also, Hansard HL 17 & 24.7.1986, cols. 1057 and 450 respectively). The Under-Secretary of State's '...remarkable lack of enthusiasm' (see Hansard HC Deb 7.12.1981, col. 680, David Waddington MP) about these Regulations in emphasising that they were: '...Community obligation(s) assumed as long ago as 1977 and 1978' was clearly noted. However, the intentions of the former Labour administration, who introduced this legislation during its British Presidency of the then European Community, were defended by

Harold Walker MP, the then Shadow spokesman. He noted that the delay between 1977 and 1981 was in fact Conservative-made and deliberate, so as to produce a: 'butchered version' of the directive. He maintained that the: '…vague, open-ended, and ill-defined, economic, technical or organisational reasons [used to] dismiss an employee' would undermine the legislation. Even the long-standing eurosceptic Teddy Taylor MP recognised the inherent uncertainties in the law as well as its deficiencies when he warned that a company might '…not worry about the agreements made between the employer and employee prior to the transfer' and ignore the legislation. In fact he summed up the ultimate danger that employers might even '…tear it up'.

Such widespread attempted evasion of the TUPE Regulations, either by design or ignorance or confusion, has in fact occurred, as is evident from the numerous cases brought in litigation. Thus, from this hurried and late enactment, the TUPE Regulations emerged and have since produced both a political and legal minefield for business transfers. The intensity of the debate is typified by Lord Wedderburn's contribution in the House of Lords debate on the introduction of the TUPE Regulations in 1981; his lordship stated that: '[These Regulations] …snatch away the rights which were intended by the Directive, like some bicycle thief snatching purses in the night' (see Hansard HL Deb 10.12.1981, col. 1490). Wedderburn's foresight recognised the numerous loopholes which the anomalies between the ARD and TUPE created.

After nearly 21 years of TUPE and the original 1977 ARD, in 1998 the Amending Directive was agreed and newly Revised TUPE Regulations will have to be enacted by July 2001. To that end, another parliamentary tranposition is awaited (this will be discussed later in Chapter 7).

Summary

This chapter has set out the historical development of the law relating to business transfers. Such a history highlights its controversial pathway into the twenty-first century, as well as providing an explanation of both the reasons why the EU decided to legislate in this area and the cause of UK problems with this European regulatory framework.

To sum up, the purpose of the EC and UK provisions are to protect employees in the event of the sale of a business, to ensure that the purchaser takes over existing contracts and liabilities, and to render any resultant dismissals unfair (unless justified – see later chapters).

A 'business transfer' (transfer of undertaking) involves the transfer of any trade or business, albeit a transfer of a discrete part of an undertaking (either geographic or functional) or a transfer in two or more stages/generations; however, it does *not* require the transfer of property. In the event of a transfer, in order to transfer, a person must be employed by the transferor, or in a complex group of structures or service companies, must be assigned to the undertaking or part transferred. Why 1977? Because a report was issued by a Committee of Experts which identified high amounts of business transfer activity, an the consequential 1974 Social Action Plan linked business transfer activity to other social legislation such as equal pay, redundancies and equal treatment.

In brief, the central terms are:

- transferor = current/former employer;

- transferee = new employer/purchaser;

- transfer = sale of a business with assets *not* shares.

Above all, the primary aims of the 1977 and 1998 Directives were to protect employees against dismissal in the event that the business changes ownership and to transfer all pre-existing terms and conditions of employment to the new employer, and in addition to enable consultation with employee representatives before the transfer on the social, legal and economic implications of the transfer. The ARD was revised in 1998 because of the identified weaknesses in the 1977 law, then out of date, and because of the increase in business transfers and emerging legal loopholes.

In the next chapter we examine the legal framework governing UK business transfers.

CHAPTER 2

The legal framework

In the last chapter the social, economic and political context of the law relating to business transfers was introduced. In this chapter, an examination of the provisions contained in both the ARD and TUPE will be undertaken in order to explain the legal conflict between these two frameworks.

Acquiring rights – the original Directive

The EU regulation on business transfers seeks to safeguard employee's rights in the event of business reorganisations, rights which the ECJ summarised in *Wendleboe* (1985) as '...to ensure, as far as possible, that the employment relationship continues unchanged with the transferee and by protecting workers against dismissals motivated solely by the fact of the transfer'. This text has already observed that the Acquired Rights Directive (ARD) became part of EC law in 1977 (see Appendix 1), but it was not implemented into UK law until 1982. Following concessions made at the 1998 Cardiff EU Summit, the British Presidency of the EU was able to secure an agreed amended draft of a revised ARD which was enacted in late 1998 and is now due to come into force in 2001. Consequently, a revised form of TUPE had to be enacted.

Articles 1 and 2 of the original 1977 ARD concern its scope and definitions. Article 1 applies to the transfer of an undertaking, or part of an undertaking, as a result of a legal transfer within the territorial scope of the EU. Article 2 provides the necessary working definitions of the central terms: 'transferor' meaning the person who ceases to be the employer and 'transferee' meaning the person who becomes the employer (as noted in Chapter 1). Article 3 sets out the aims of the Directive. The integral purpose of the ARD is that the transferor's rights, obligations and liabilities arising from the contract of employment existing on the date of the business transfer are transferred to the transferee and that the transferee shall continue to observe those terms and conditions, collective agreements and any pre-existing trade union recognition. The only exception to the rule is contained in Article 3(3) which stipulates that such provisions shall not cover old-age, invalidity or survivor's benefits or any other pensions.

Central to this secondary legislation are Articles 4 to 6 which seek to *safeguard employees' rights*. Article 4 declares that a business transfer cannot result in dismissal or redundancy, except where such dismissals are for economic, technical or organisational (ETO) reasons. These defences will be discussed in detail in Chapter 6 as HR solutions. Where an employee is dismissed or made redundant prior to a business transfer, then the 'new' employer, the transferee, shall be regarded as having been responsible for termination of the contract. Article 5 asserts that the primary aim of the ARD is to preserve the employees' rights post-transfer. In terms of consultation, Article 6 requires the parties to the business transfer, the transferor and transferee, to inform and consult their employees, or their recognised unions, giving the reasons for the business transfer, and explaining the legal, economic and social implications of the business transfer, as well as the envisaged effects to those employees of the transfer, this consultation being undertaken 'in good time' prior to the transfer and 'with a view to seeking agreement'. These obligations may be restricted to either trade unions only, or alternatively, to individual employees only (these consultation issues will be considered in Chapter 5 in detail).

Articles 7 to 10 involve the *enforcement and implementation* of the Directive. The EU Council addressed the Directive to *all* Member States who were obliged to bring these provisions into force within two years. Once enacted such national legislation should be registered with the EU Commission in order for the EU Commission to submit the legislation to the EU Council for confirmation. While the ARD lays down the minimum provisions to be adopted, it does allow EU Member States to introduce more favourable laws to employees than the requirements set out above.

The UK's pre-existing law before TUPE 1981

Prior to the ARD, UK common law provided a less sophisticated legal framework. An employee had no freedom of contract when a change of employer, by way of a transfer of a business, had taken place. At common law, a business transfer bringing about a change in ownership resulted in the automatic termination of a contract of employment giving rise to a dismissal, which entitled employees to claim wrongful dismissal, a redundancy payment or compensation for unfair dismissal. Section 141 of ERA 1996 granted employers a defence to redundancy when an offer to renew the employment arose before the transfer actually took place. If an employee accepted such an offer, then no dismissal took place and an employee was precluded from obtaining a redundancy payment, although if the employee was offered suitable employment and the employee unreasonably refused, such a rejection would forfeit a redundancy payment claim.

Lord Atkin in the *Nokes* case commented that despite all of the common law's shortcomings in relation to business transfers, '…the servant was left with his inalienable right to choose whether he would serve a new master or not', a choice which meant that freedom of contract was retained in the employment relationship. Similarly, the EAT in its decision in *Woods* v. *WM Car Services (Peterborough) Limited* in 1981 observed the new owners of the business reneging on their original agreement to preserve existing terms and conditions of employees and offering employees lower wages and longer hours. Woods rejected the new terms and was dismissed. The case turned on whether constructive dismissal could be found. The EAT, agreeing with the IT, found that constructive dismissal could not be established since it is implied in a contract of employment that employers will not without proper cause act to damage the employment relationship. The employee's appeal was subsequently dismissed by the Court of Appeal. Since the TUPE

Regulations did not come into force in the UK until 1982, this case demonstrates what behaviour the ARD was intended to prevent, which Browne-Wilkinson J alluded to in his judgment in *Woods*.

The ARD and TUPE, in a British context, marked a departure from the rigid common law doctrine of privity of contract, a doctrine which justified dismissals and no continuity of employment when the ownership of a business changed. This doctrine had been challenged by s. 218 of ERA 1996. The pre-1982 common law is now, of course, superseded by the TUPE Regulations. TUPE has often been criticised for limiting the freedom of employers to arrange both their contractual and commercial affairs so as to minimise their employment law liabilities. The next section of this text will examine those criticisms by evaluating the current TUPE framework.

TUPE Regulations 1981

From the perspective of the early 1990s, employment law is predominantly a statutory subject, set, no doubt, in a common law context and subject to the vagaries of judicial interpretation, and the main engine of its development has been legislative rather than judicial. In the case of business transfers, a statutory accommodation of the Directive was drafted, implemented and interpreted by the judiciary in the UK. The UK has implemented its obligations arising from the ARD in its TUPE Regulations 1981. These Regulations, which came into force in 1982, aimed to ensure that once a business transfer was proposed, employers would consult and inform employees, as well as provide for the transfer of the contracts of employment of the employees affected by the business transfer. The TUPE Regulations were supposed to fully implement the ARD (see Appendix 2), as required under s. 2 of the European Communities Act 1972. Subsequently, Regulations 1 to 3 and 10 to 13 came into force on 1 February 1982, whereas Regulations 4 to 9 and 14 came into operation after 1 May 1982. They were amended in 1993 by s. 33, TURERA, in 1995 by the Terms and Conditions of Employment (Collective Redundancies and Transfers of Undertakings) Regulations and again in 1996 by s. 218 of ERA. These Regulations were further amended in 1999, and these will be considered later in Chapter 5.

Regulation 1 allows for the Regulations to be cited and declares the dates when they came into force while Regulation 2(1) establishes definitions in order to assist the usage of these Regulations. A wide definition of employee is provided, since it includes anyone who works for another, except an independent contractor. The essential term 'undertaking' is defined as 'any trade or business'. Originally this excluded any undertaking or part thereof which is not in the nature of a commercial venture, but following TURERA's amendment to Regulation 2(1), an undertaking now includes any non-commercial trade or business. Regulation 2(2) provides for part of an undertaking, including separate, severable or self-contained, to be an identifiable part of the business as a whole so as to be transferred. Despite all of these definitions, the Regulations are limited and they exclude certain types of employment, for example overseas employees (Regulation 13(1)).

The central concept upon which the Regulations rely is that there must be a 'relevant transfer', as defined in Regulation 3. This concept is defined as a transfer of an undertaking or part of an undertaking situated in the UK (Regulation 2(1)). The EAT in *Premier Motors (Medway) Ltd* v. *Total Oil of Great Britain Ltd* (1984) held that under the Regulations a transfer was considered the same as a change in the ownership of the business, whereas the ECJ's approach believes that the directive is more far-reaching and is not limited solely to a change in ownership. TURERA's amendment to Regulation 3(4) clarifies that a transfer takes place irrespective of whether or not any property is transferred.

The 'going concern' test established in *Kenmir Ltd* v. *Frizzell* (1968) to determine whether a business is being transferred has regard to the substance of the transfer rather than its form, given consideration to the whole of the circumstances. The vital factor is whether the effect of the business transfer means that the business transferred 'could carry on without interruption'. This test was approved in *Lloyd* v. *Brassey* (1969) where Lord Denning MR asked 'Does the business remain the same business but in different hands?' Similarly, in *Spijkers* case (1986) the ECJ held it necessary to find an 'economic entity' following a transfer for there to be a relevant business transfer. The 'economic entity' test, as it has become known, has been widely applied to several circumstances since 1986. In particular, it was applied in the ECJ's rulings in the *Redmond* (1992) and *Rask* (1993) cases. However, this remains a question of fact for the IT to decide. A 'relevant' business transfer applies only to a transfer of undertaking and not a takeover by means of share transfer.

Regulation 4 provides for business transfers by receivers or liquidators. Thus, where an administrator or receiver transfers the company or part of the company's undertaking to a wholly owned subsidiary of the company, this will not be deemed a business transfer until the transferee's company ceases to be wholly owned by the transferor. Regulation 4 has no such equivalent provision in the ARD. The ECJ held that the ARD was inapplicable to insolvency. Subsequently the ECJ held that the ARD did apply in restricted circumstances where the purpose was to protect the assets of the business from the creditors and allow the business to continue trading.

The *Spence* case (*Secretary of State for Employment* v. *Spence* (1986)) illustrated the problematical 'prior to transfer' position of the legislation with regard to liquidation. This case involved receivership of a company where the Secretary of State was the custodian because of the liability as prescribed by the redundancy fund. However, once the business was sold the employees were re-employed. The dispute arose out of the fact that the Secretary of State claimed that the liability was transferred to the transferee under Regulation 5 of the 1981 Regulations and the contracts were not terminated as was founded in *Nokes*, the common law which the 1981 Regulations had overruled. The Secretary of State contended that Regulation 5(3) applied Regulation 5(1) to contracts not only existing at the moment of business transfer, but those terminated immediately before, relying upon *Apex Leisure Hire* v. *Barrat* (1984). The Court of Appeal held that Regulation 5(1) applied. A contract which had already been terminated by the transferor could not be terminated again by the business transfer. Subsequently, Regulation 4 was amended in 1987 in order to provide for the preservation of the receiver's or liquidator's freedom as contained in the Insolvency Act 1986 when attempting to sell the business as a 'going concern', the latter practice being known as 'hiving-off' or 'hiving-down'. The transfer by the receiver or liquidator to the subsidiary company was not to be treated immediately as a 'relevant transfer'. Regulations 4(1)(a) and (b) apply where the ultimate transferee acquires the undertaking by the transfer of shares in the subsidiary company and then a 'relevant business transfer' emerges. This amended provision solely ensures that the business transfer is actually only suspended.

In respect of receivership, the House of Lords in *Litster* (1989), a case involving the dismissal of an entire workforce one hour before going into receivership, held that liability for these dismissals passed to the transferee because these workers were 'employed immediately before the transfer' under Regulation 5(3). An exception to the general application of the Regulations continues to be advanced with regard to insolvency-related business transfers. The ECJ in *Wendleboe v. LJ Musik Aps (In Liquidation)* (1986) presented the question whether Article 3(1) of the Directive required EU Member States to enact provisions which would transfer a vendor's obligations to his former employees and those employed at the moment of business transfer. It was held that there was no need for enactment because it was '... doubtful whether the Regulations would improve the position of the employees.' The advantages of automatic termination for the transferee are that they are free of legal obligations and are able to selectively re-engage former employees. This selective re-engagement is made illegal by the 1981 Regulations because they provide for their automatic transfer, while Regulation 8(1) protects employees from unfair dismissal, although Regulation 8(2), the 'Economic, Technical and Organisational' (ETO) defences, preserve the employer's freedom. The decision in *Spence* deprives employees of certain benefits which were conferred by the Regulations, most notably basic pay as provided for in the redundancy fund, as well as no compensatory award in unfair dismissal claims.

Furthermore, the protection provided to employees by the Court of Appeal in *Berriman* v. *Delabole Slate Ltd* (1985), that of the right to constructive dismissal in a transfer situation, is undercut by these ETO defences. The *Spence* case has often been seen as an unwelcome decision, since the Court of Appeal fails to grasp that if a contract is not transferred then the liability for terminating it is so transferred by Regulation 5(2). This was highlighted in the *Litster* decision which conflicts with the ECJ in *Wendelboe*. Under Regulation 5(2)(a) the transferee is liable in respect of termination of the contract before dismissal. However, such a situation gives substance to Regulation 5(3). On the other hand, in *Berriman* the employer's rights to unilaterally change terms and conditions were removed, but this has now been restored by *Spence*.

The effects of a business transfer on contracts of employment are dealt with in Regulation 5 which provides for the passing of all the rights, powers, duties and liabilities under the contract of employment post-transfer. Regulation 5(5) gives rise to the right of any employee to terminate the contract of employment without notice if there is a substantial and detrimental change to the working conditions. Regulation 6 provides for the post-transfer of existing collective agreements made with recognised trade unions on behalf of employees whose contracts of employment are preserved by Regulation 5(1). Regulation 7 provides for the anomalous exclusion of occupational pensions in any contracts which were transferred or to any rights, duties or liabilities which relate in any agreements to occupational pension schemes.

Fundamental to the TUPE framework is Regulation 8 which provides protection from dismissal either prior or post-transfer. Should dismissal occur, then the affected employees are granted protection under Part X and s. 218 of ERA 1996 for unfair dismissal with the business transfer as the reason or principal reason for their dismissal. Such dismissals will be deemed unfair, unless the reason for the dismissal is based on ETO grounds and this can be supported by changes brought about either by the transferee or transferor, either prior or post-transfer. Presently these defences have not resulted in causing much of the litigation surrounding TUPE in the UK. However, so important are these defences that this thesis anticipates that the future debate and litigation surrounding the ETO justifications will be the next important issue for the courts to address.

Trade union recognition is affirmed in Regulation 9, conditional upon the fact that there is a 'relevant transfer'. The duty to inform and consult recognised trade unions in 'long enough time before a relevant transfer to enable consultations to take place' is provided for in accordance with the Directive's guidance. Such consultation or information should confirm that the transfer is to take place and when, and the reasons for it, the legal, economic and social implications of the business transfer, and the measures envisaged in connection with the business transfer, in writing and by post. Furthermore, the transferee is required to give the transferor all the information agreed. Employees are given the right to consult their trade unions and their unions are required to consider affected employees' representations, the whole practice being undertaken on the premise that such be 'reasonably practicable'. Consequently, should the employer fail to inform or consult then the trade union concerned can present a complaint to an Employment Tribunal. The ECJ's ruling in *Wren* (1993) reiterates that Regulation 10 invokes the question of the 'reasonably practicable' circumstances of the situation in which the employer was expected to perform such tasks as consultation and 'seeking agreement' with the workforce on the business transfer. If the ET deems the employer to be in breach of those duties imposed in Regulation 10, then it will order a compensatory award of four weeks' pay. It is worth noting that any agreements shall be deemed void if they seek to exclude or restrict Regulations 5, 8 or 10, or prevent any person from presenting a complaint to an ET. Regulations 8, 10 and 11 are inapplicable to those employed abroad (i.e. outside the UK or who are ordinarily employees on board a ship outside the UK, despite the ship being registered in the UK) or as dock workers. Regulation 14 allows for any consequential amendments to the Regulations.

These controversial Regulations have fuelled much of the litigation and debate about the effectiveness of the laws on business transfers. Many of these cases have seriously questioned whether the TUPE Regulations have adequately implemented the ARD. The current case law shows that this objective is being subverted by arguments framed centrally around Regulations 4, 5 and 8, in order to evade the duties imposed by the Regulations. Furthermore, the weak provisions central to protecting employees, consultation and information, particularly Regulations 10 and 11, demonstrate how ineffective the TUPE regulatory framework really is.

EU–UK legal conflict: the legislative anomalies

It is clear from the chapters of this book that the 1977 Acquired Rights Directive sits uneasily between the EU's policy on labour in the enterprise and the free labour market policy of the common market origins of the EU. The existence of two legislative instruments resulted in many anomalies prevailing which arose out of the ill-transposition of these EU obligations into UK law. These anomalies from 1981 have caused much confusion because of the uncertainty surrounding these provisions, accompanied by the UK government's and the courts' failure to properly clarify issues. This failure of both government and legal system has resulted in the UK government seeking to regulate business reorganisations by way of secondary legislation under its contracting-out policies. As the 1982 TUPE Regulations and the ARD did not coincide, I will observe that these anomalies were intended to be resolved by s. 33 of TURERA 1993.

It remains a true observation that the TUPE Regulations in part go beyond and in other quarters narrow the strict letter of the ARD. For example, the TUPE Regulations apply to voluntary and involuntary business transfers, whereas the ARD referred only to voluntary business transfers ('involuntary' means those brought about by financial reasons, such as bankruptcy, as opposed to 'voluntary' which connotes consent, agreement and choice). Secondly, the requirement under the ARD to inform and consult workers, pursuant to Article 6, is given an escape route in the TUPE Regulations under Regulation 10(7), in terms of an exemption clause drafted on the basis of 'not reasonably practicable' grounds; the ARD has no equivalent. Article 3, with regard to the scope of the directive, is narrowed in Regulation 5 which limits the effect of the business transfer to rights and duties as contained in the contract of employment as opposed to the employment relationship existing on the date of a business transfer. Lastly, Regulation 8 provides defences for those employers who dismiss as a result of business transfers either prior to or after the business transfer, with good reason so to do on economic, technical or organisational grounds.

The question of conformity has been considered in two EAT decisions: firstly, in *Robert Seligman Corporation* v. *Baker* (1983) it was acknowledged, in considering whether there was a business transfer, that in the event of future ambiguity between TUPE and the ARD it would be presumed that TUPE must conform to the requirements of the ARD. This meant that the ARD would prevail and TUPE read as if the ARD was transposed word for word. The Scottish EAT in *Meikle* v. *McPhail (Charleston Arms)* (1983), considering Regulation 8, contended that TUPE did not accurately reflect the ARD. These two cases highlight how the Scottish and English EATs have reached different conclusions using the same legislation and shows the uncertainty which surrounds the TUPE Regulations. Perhaps this also demonstrates why the current uncertainty exists, when in fact the courts cannot agree among themselves as to whether the ARD or TUPE prevails. By way of resolution of this dispute, it has become customary practice for the British courts to take the TUPE Regulations as they find them. Only, in circumstances of ambiguity must the ARD be used for interpretation purposes.

The purposive interpretation given to the TUPE Regulations to ensure their consistency with the ARD was considered by their Lordships in the *Duke* v. *GEC* (1988) and *Pickstone* v. *Freemans*

(1988) cases. In *Duke*, the House of Lords, in determining the applicability of the Equal Treatment Directive, declined reliance upon the accompanying regulations. Similarly, the House of Lords in the *Pickstone* case gave effect to the Equal Treatment Directive by importing wording into the Equal Pay (Amendment) Regulations 1983 in order to make them consistent with the directive. Applying this reasoning to business transfers, the House of Lords in *Litster* v. *Forth Dry Dock Engineering Ltd* (1989) implied words into Regulation 5(3) of TUPE in order to allow the employees' claims for unfair dismissal which otherwise would have been ineffective. As the House of Lords ruled, per Lord Templeman: 'The Courts of the UK are under a duty to follow the practice of the ECJ by giving a purposive construction to Directives and to Regulations issued for the purpose of complying with Directives'. For over a decade, the lack of compatibility between TUPE and the ARD has persisted.

EU infraction proceedings and TURERA's amendments 1993

As a result of these anomalies the EU Commission in November 1992 initiated infringement proceedings against the UK government for not fully complying with its obligations under s. 2(2) of the European Communities Act (ECA) 1972. The EU Commission's actions were provoked by a Report which examined EU Member States' treatment of the ARD. The Report outlined five salient problem areas in the UK: *firstly*, the exclusion of non-commercial undertakings; *secondly*, the sanctions for non-compliance were inadequate; *thirdly*, consultation with workers did not aim to seek agreement, but merely to inform; *fourthly*, the appointment of worker's representatives was being evaded because of the growing British obsession with union derecognition; and *lastly*, the restrictive British requisite that the transferor must be the owner of the undertaking.

These criticisms, which had been made earlier in 1988 in a Report for the EU Commission undertaken by Professors Byre and Hepple, showed that the inconsistency in the UK courts and tribunals, as already explained, was making it difficult for employers and employees alike, as well as UK lawyers, to establish what rights, liabilities and risks were involved with business transfers. The UK government's reaction to these proceedings was to reject these alleged breaches of duties, while simultaneously agreeing to change the law accordingly. In 1993, due to the EU Commission's renewed threats to initiate infraction proceedings against the British government, TURERA was enacted as a set of statutory provisions which aimed to curtail the EU Commission's pending proceedings. TURERA amended Regulations 3 and 5 so as to allow more than one transaction to be transferred and to accommodate the right to refuse a business transfer which results in the employee's contract not being transferred. It also strengthened Regulations 10 and 11 to ensure that the duty to consult is executed 'with a view to seeking their agreement' and increased the sanction for non-compliance from two to four weeks' pay. These detailed reforms illustrate the government's previous failure to comply. The success of the EU Commission's infraction proceedings against the UK before the ECJ acknowledged the UK government's consistent reluctance to modify TUPE and initiated talks at the EU level with regard to revising the

ARD. Subsequently, the EU Commission's 1992 Report resulted in intra-EU discussion about revision of the ARD in order to clarify its original intentions to protect workers.

The controversy surrounding the ARD has been fuelled further by recent ECJ decisions impacting on contracting out. The latest infraction action by the EU Commission against the UK, albeit in relation to the law prior to TURERA's amendments, vindicated those commentators and unions who had maintained that TUPE was incompatible with the ARD. The ECJ ruled, considering the criticisms of TUPE already given, that the UK had failed to fulfil its obligations under, *inter alia*, the ARD by its exclusion of non-profit-making undertakings from TUPE, although Article 1(1) of the ARD makes no such distinction. Section 33 of TURERA 1993 amended Regulation 2(1) of the TUPE Regulations and deleted the reference to the exclusion of non-commercial undertakings. The ECJ applied the directive to non-commercial organisations, for instance a drug addicts recovery charity, which brought the TUPE Regulations in line with EU jurisprudence. Despite this amendment, the other anomalies previously discussed remained. For example, Article 6 of the ARD provides for worker representatives to be consulted by their employers so as to 'seek agreement' prior to being subjected to a business transfer, though Regulation 10, until its amendment under s. 33 of TURERA 1993, did not contain such a provision. Arguably the UK government has met most of the court's criticisms with its enactment of TURERA 1993, but the outstanding 'Francovich' actions – actions supported by UK unions against the British government for its failure to implement the ARD fully – denotes that the reluctant passing of

TURERA has still failed to transpose its obligations under the ARD completely. The ECJ has on four occasions condemned EU Member States for their failure to implement the ARD properly.

The ECJ in *EC Commission* v. *Belgium* (1988) stated that the implementation of the ARD should not diminish employees' existing rights. Once TUPE was implemented the pre-existing right to decline a business transfer to the transferee was lost, although the later ruling of the ECJ in *Katsikas* v. *Konstantinidis* (1988), involving an employee's refusal to be transferred, does reiterate that employees have the right to claim constructive dismissal should they disagree with the business transfer. In this case, a German waiter refused to work for another local restaurateur he disliked to whom his former employer had sold his restaurant. Such a right to refuse does indirectly preserve the doctrine of freedom of contract between the employer and the employee subjected to the business transfer. This right to refuse a business transfer reaffirms the proposition that 'labour is *not* a commodity' and so it rejects the market as a sole determinant. A last-minute amendment to Regulation 5(4) by s. 33 of TURERA provides that an employee may inform the transferor or transferee that they object to the business transfer which will result in the employee not being transferred with the undertaking. Exercising such objection therefore results in the termination of the contract of employment, which realistically means that the employee becomes unemployed and faced with such a fate has no substantive, enforceable rights to complain about, in the individual employee's view, an unfavourable business transfer.

According to the Scottish EAT in *Hay* v. *George Hanson (Building Contractors) Ltd* (1996) an objection is construed as a refusal to accept the business transfer. Mr Hay, a joiner with Argyll and Bute District Council, was unhappy about transferring to George Hanson, a building contractor. Lord Johnston observed that, since the drafting of the TUPE Regulations was silent on this issue, then such refusals to be transferred, objections, were to be determined on the particular circumstances of the case. Reflecting upon '…the draconian nature of…Regulation 5(4B)…' of TUPE, the EAT relied upon established EC law as laid out in its ruling in *Katsikas*. It noted that an informed objection to a transfer shall be treated as a self-termination of the contract of employment between the employee and the transferor and his successor, the transferee. It was further qualified by the ECJ in *Merckx* v. *Ford Motors Co.* (1996) to be discussed in detail below. In *Merckx*, the ECJ ruling on the second issue concerning whether the employees' refusal of the business transfer due to the lack of guarantees about existing pay levels being maintained after the business transfer stated that it was a matter for domestic law to determine what should happen to the contract of employment should the employee object to the business transfer. Consequently, the UK stance has chosen to provide for constructive dismissal in such circumstances, as the case of *Hay* v. *George Hanson (Building Contractors) Ltd* (1996) clearly demonstrates.

In *Hay* the EAT held that any employee's objection must be brought to the attention of the transferor or transferee, either orally or by way of action, before the date of transfer. A further curious development created by the UK courts prevails in the EAT's ruling in *Photostatic Copiers (Southern) Ltd* v. *Okuda and Japan Office Equipment Ltd (in Liquidation)* (1995). The EAT's decision resurrects the common law principle of 'novation of the contract'. In this case, the EAT upheld the IT's decision that the applicant, Mr Okuda, continued to be employed until informed otherwise by his employers or unless he resigned. The EAT reminded the transferor and transferee that a business transfer does not take effect until the employee is given notice of both the fact of the business transfer and the identity of the transferee. Judge Peppitt QC's reliance upon the common law principle of novation of the contract which requires the consent of the employee resulted in the EAT choosing to ignore previous ECJ rulings (see ruling in *Berg & Busschers* v. *Besselsen* (1989)) and stating that no employee consent is required in respect of business transfers. The EAT accepted that the employer should be informed of the employee's objection, albeit a pointless gesture since the consequences facing the employee were more severe than those for the employer who only had to find a replacement employee.

In terms of detrimental loss the directive has direct effect in that it can be relied on against an EU Member State or an emanation of a State. In terms of loss, the ECJ in *Francovich* v. *Italian Republic* (1992) has definitively stated that an EU Member State may be liable to pay damages where it has failed to properly implement EC law. For such claims to be successful, three conditions have to be satisfied: firstly, that the rights lost are determined by the directive; secondly, that the directive confers rights for an individual's benefit; and lastly, that a causal link can be established between the breach of a State's obligations and the damage suffered. The latter is the most difficult to prove and this is where most of these claims are expected to fail.

The *EC Commission* v. *UK* (1994) case, concerning consultation rights when subjected to a business transfer, shows that, despite the

UK having been forced to make changes to TUPE in 1993, even by 1994 the UK government was condemned once more for its failure to fully implement its obligations under the ARD. This case will be discussed in detail later in Chapter 5. As a consequence of these anomalies, shortcomings and modifications, the courts, both the ECJ and in the UK, have played a significant interpretative role, if not a consistent one, so as to clarify in order to maintain the law.

The ECJ's case law

Due to the shortcomings in the ARD and EU Member States' implementing provisions, the ECJ has had no alternative but to preserve the Directive's aims. Since 1985, the ECJ has ruled over 30 times on the ARD, and further cases are awaited. The ARD has also been the subject of a number of preliminary rulings, the purpose of these ECJ rulings being to assist EU Member States with their interpretation of the obligations arising under the ARD. An important ruling from the ECJ is that of *Schmidt* (1994), where the ECJ ruled that the contracting out of a single cleaner came within the scope of the ARD and so could be transferred. In particular, the absence of tangible assets and the fact that it is an ancillary activity and performed by a single employee are not decisive factors for the purpose of establishing a transfer. The significance of *Schmidt* is the ECJ's conclusion that the retention of its identity is the decisive criterion for establishing whether a business transfer has occurred. In support of this is Advocate-General Van Gerven's question '...whether the cessation of a specific operation within an undertaking and the consequent transfer of that operation to an outside undertaking is to be regarded as a transfer of a part of the undertaking within the meaning of the Directive?' An answer to this question is given by the ECJ in *Schmidt* which held contracting-out to be clearly within the scope of the ARD. Previously in *Rask* (1993), a case concerning the tendering out of the operational running of a canteen service, the ECJ had reaffirmed the 'retention of identity' test and categorically included contracting-out (CCT) within the ARD.

The ECJ's growing jurisprudence has been immensely active in clarifying the ARD. In particular, the ECJ's ruling in *Spijkers* (1986), which established the criteria for identifying 'a legal transfer', played a significant role in the development of the law relating to business transfers. The ECJ's rulings in *Redmond* (including public and private undertakings under the ambit of the ARD), *Rask* (including business transfers brought about by contracting out within the scope of the ARD) and *Katsikas* (already discussed, granting employees a right to resign should they disagree with the business transfer) highlight the growing important influence of EC law in this area.

As already discussed the *Schmidt* judgment met with strong criticism from many EU governments. In particular, some German lawyers refused to accept that an activity can be transferred without a transfer of goodwill and business knowledge. This ECJ ruling strongly influenced the UK courts in the *Dines* case. Fuelling the controversy surrounding the scope of the ARD, the ECJ's ruling in the *Rygaard* case (1995), concerning a firm of carpenters who were contracted to construct a canteen, contains some of the German disapproval of the *Schmidt* ruling. In *Rygaard*, following the bankruptcy of the main contractor, the carpenters who had been made redundant as a consequence were transferred to the subcontractor to complete the work. Ole Rygaard, one of the carpenters affected, sought damages for wrongful dismissal. Considering all the facts and applying the ECJ's previous ruling in *Spijkers*, the ECJ, disagreeing with the Advocate-General, held that there was no transfer where one undertaking merely made available to another certain workers and materials for carrying out particular works. The ECJ reasoned that the making available of workers and materials did not constitute a stable economic activity as no assets had been transferred. Thus such a failure meant that certain activities formerly undertaken by the transferor could not be transferred. This ruling suggests that the ECJ might be retreating from its earlier position in the *Schmidt* ruling.

The ECJ's ruling in *Merckx*, concerning the transfer of a single-area dealership to another dealer, restated the Court's reasoning in *Schmidt* that one person is sufficient for a transfer, as is one entity. In *Merckx*, two salesmen sued Ford when it had discontinued its dealership held by their employer Anfo Motors, having passed it over to another independent dealer, Novarobel. Novarobel took on only 14 of Anfo's 64 existing employees. The business transfer also incurred a change in location. In the ECJ's view, no contractual relationship between the parties was necessary for a business transfer. Thus, following this reasoning, the ECJ held that any replacement of an outgoing contractor by a successful, incoming contractor is a relevant business transfer and one which is covered by the ARD. In this case the ECJ ruled that the employees had a right to object to the business transfer and claim compensation in circumstances where they were being compelled to change employer and take up employment on worse terms and conditions. Returning to its orthodox position the ECJ in *Merckx* found that the ARD applied, despite there being no contractual link between the transferor and transferee and no passing of tangible assets.

It can be contended that the significance of the ECJ's ruling in *Rygaard* marks a retreat towards more conservative approaches than those seen by the ECJ in terms of its other rulings on business transfers since 1985. The ECJ in *Merckx*, however, confined the *Rygaard* ruling to the facts of its particular case, by finding that a change of workplace and name did not prevent the ARD from applying. Thus a business transfer occurs where a stable economic entity exists, irrespective of the contractual relationship. Until recently, the ECJ, it could have been argued, had regained its enthusiasm for business transfers by reviving its 'robust' stance in *Merckx*. In its most recent rulings, *Henke* (1996) and *Suzen* (1997), the ECJ has returned to its conservative reservations about CCT, as witnessed in *Rygaard*.

In *Henke*, a case concerning the reorganisation of municipal administration, the ECJ held that legal secretaries and other administrative staff working for local authorities in Germany could be dismissed or have their terms and conditions changed as a consequence of a business transfer between a former local authority and a contractor. In this terse ruling by the ECJ, Mrs Henke's dismissal as a mayor's secretary when the municipal administration was transferred to the regional authority could now open the floodgates and allow many contracting-out exercises involving administrative staff to avoid the ARD. The ECJ's reasoning was based on the failure of these administrative workers to hold a stable economic entity, as service providers, to constitute a business transfer. Such a ruling has wide-ranging implications for many of the contracting-out scenarios, unless the decision in *Henke* is narrowly read to be applicable only to those activities which are administrative and not wholly economic in nature.

Similarly, the ECJ in *Suzen* argued that a cleaning contract to clean a church-run secondary school in Bonn, which was terminated with one contractor and awarded to another giving rise to eight dismissals on the grounds of redundancy, did not by the mere fact that the service provided by the old and new contractor was similar support the conclusion that a business transfer had taken place. In his Opinion Advocate-General La Pergola went further and contended that the transfer of a bare service contract from an outgoing to an incoming contractor, where no tangible or intangible assets were passing, did not constitute a business transfer within the scope of the ARD.

The ECJ held in *Suzen* that a transfer of activities was insufficient to amount to a transfer of an undertaking. Rejecting the Advocate-General's opinion, the ECJ reaffirmed the orthodox 'economic entity' test which had been developed in *Spijkers* and later refined in *Schmidt* and *Merckx*. Thus, no relationship need exist between the transferor and transferee prior to the transfer for the ARD to apply, but the passing of tangible assets or the taking over of a workforce remain as prerequisites for meeting the *Spijkers* test. Had the ECJ followed the Advocate-General's advice, the *Suzen* decision would have impacted on all contracted labour-only services. What is interesting from a British perspective is that the

Suzen case directly conflicts with the EAT's approach adopted in *Birch* v. *Nuneaton & Bedworth Borough Council* (1995), where the transfer of the Council's leisure facilities to an external contractor, who was responsible for actually providing similar activities, albeit in different hands, was sufficient to amount to a business transfer as the identity of the undertaking is retained. Such conflict leaves the UK courts in a quandary, although the Court of Appeal, upholding the supremacy of EC law, recently followed the *Suzen* ruling in its decision in the *Betts* case, discussed below in detail. However, it remains a salient fact that, despite this recent legal conservatism on the part of the ECJ, had the ECJ adhered to the Advocate-General's Opinion in *Suzen* the court's narrowing of the scope of the ARD would have been advanced more radically than at present. In any event, it can be contended that the *Schmidt* ruling remains the high-water mark on the ARD's application, since except for *Henke*, *Suzen* and *Rygaard*, which it could be argued are rulings confined to their facts, the ECJ's jurisprudence since 1985 has been one which has emphasised their concern about defending the ARD's primary purpose: to protect employees subject to business transfers.

The ECJ's latest rulings, *Sanchez Hildago* (1999) and *Collino* (2000) (to be discussed in Chapter 6), do very little, except remind all concerned with business transfers that employees subjected to a business transfer are transferred automatically by the mere fact of the transfer and thus, from that moment onwards, the employees are legally employed by the transferee. It thus follows from this sacrosanct principle of automatic transfer that contracts of employment transfer as a matter of law, irrespective of whether the employer or employee knows that a business transfer has occurred.

Some UK decisions on TUPE

The caseload of business transfer litigation has been ever increasing since 1989. Somewhat like Lord Denning's infamous 'incoming tide', not only has the common law developed at EU level, but at domestic level the pace of litigation has also been rapid. This is reflected in Scott Baker J's statement in the *Betts* case at first instance: 'I cannot believe that the legal position is so finely tuned that laymen cannot normally tell from the outset whether TUPE applies.' In response to that statement, it is the legal confusion surrounding TUPE which has caused much of the litigation.

The UK courts' most important TUPE ruling on business transfers was that delivered by the House of Lord's ruling in *Litster*. Since 1989, *Litster* has provided a timely reminder that the ARD seeks to safeguard employees' rights, when subjected to business transfers. Their Lordships held in *Litster* that the 'UK courts are under a duty to give a purposive construction to Directives and to Regulations issued for the purpose of complying with Directives'. As in the *Dines* case, the *Litster* decision clearly exposes a fundamental clash of philosophies between domestic and Community laws, particularly in respect of contracting out. The Court of Appeal in *Dines*, provides authoritative confirmation that the contracting out of services, including a change of contractor as a result of a CCT exercise, will usually be covered by TUPE.

Chapter 1 opened with a discussion of the important case concerning Mrs Dines. This landmark case will now be considered in detail. Mrs Dines and others initiated proceedings in the ET on the grounds of unfair dismissal by reason that both her old and new employers had failed to give effect to the TUPE Regulations 1981.

The ET concluded that since the new employer had introduced their own management, equipment, stock or supplies and because there was no transfer of goodwill between the cleaning contractors, then no business transfer had occurred. The following extract of the ET's decision was to take on a crucial significance when the case came before the Court of Appeal:

> The fact that the business is not sold does not mean that there cannot be a transfer within the meaning of the Regulations. However, when one company enters into competition with a number of other companies to obtain a contract as happened in this case and a different company wins the contract from the company that was previously providing the services then this is a cessation of the business of the first contractors on the hospital premises, and the commencement of a new business by [Pall Mall] when they are awarded the contract. The fact that [Pall Mall] employed the same workforce at the same workplace is not in this case a factor giving rise to a transfer under the Regulations for the reasons given in this decision.

The ET had decided that there had not been a complete transfer of staff and, in any event, transfer of personnel was only one factor to be taken into account. The ET concluded there had been no transfer of equipment, goodwill or other tangible assets, nor any distinctive way of working. Accordingly, the EAT rejected the suggestion that the ET had misdirected itself in any way or that its decision was perverse.

In the Court of Appeal, it was maintained that the question whether there had been a business transfer or not admitted of only an affirmative answer. Applying the criteria established in *Spijkers*, already discussed, the services consisted of the provision of labour only, the labour force remained the same, the nature and the scope of the services provided were identical, the place at which the services were undertaken was the same, and the services were provided for the same customer, namely Basildon and Thurrock Health Authority. Eventually, it was accepted in the *Dines* case that the cleaning services at the Orsett Hospital were an undertaking.

In contrast to *Dines* is the Court of Appeal's approach in *Betts* (1997), a case concerning the contracting-out of helicopter services and the redeployment of existing staff to the 'new' contractor. Their Lordships held that where the labour force was not the only asset of the operation and a vast majority of its assets were retained, it could not be said that the undertaking was transferred. In the words of Kennedy LJ: 'With the benefit of Suzen we are satisfied that the proper approach was to consider first the nature of...the operation...As to this issue...there was no transfer of the undertaking so that it retained its identity.' Thus in deciding whether an operation was an undertaking for the purposes of TUPE, the court had to look beyond the activity entrusted to it. Since in most cases there would be land, buildings, plant and staff all contributing to the undertaking, while these would be sufficient to sustain an undertaking and an economic activity, such would be insufficient for the purposes of determining whether a transfer of an undertaking has taken place. Such a juxtaposition by the Court of Appeal with its judgment in *Dines* now causes only to confuse the law further, making it harder for all concerned with business transfers within the UK to determine whether TUPE applies or not.

It appears that the progress made could now have been temporarily obscured. However, since the Court of Appeal relied upon the ECJ's ruling in *Schmidt* in *Dines*, it emerges that the only bewilderment with the ARD in the courts persists in whether to apply *Schmidt* or *Suzen* in deciding whether an undertaking is transferable for the purposes of TUPE in each individual case.

Some interesting judicial reasoning is demonstrated in two cases in the UK EAT: *Sunley Turiff Holdings Ltd* v. *Thomson* (1995) and *Michael Peters Ltd* v. *Farnfield and Michael Peters Group Plc* (1995). Here the UK courts highlight how subsidiaries, groups of companies comprising separate corporate bodies connected through share ownership, can avoid the legal regulation of business transfers. In the *Michael Peters* case, Mr Farnfield, as chief executive responsible for all 25 subsidiaries, claimed unfair dismissal when the parent company became insolvent and he was made redundant. The EAT reversed the ET's finding of unfair dismissal, as the dismissal was deemed not to be connected with the business transfer as Mr Farnfield was not employed by the transferor. The crucial consideration for the EAT was whether or not the applicant was employed in the part of the undertaking being transferred, irrespective of the insolvency of the business.

In contrast, in the *Sunley* litigation, another case involving a subsidiary company situation, the Scottish EAT considered that the dismissal of Mr Thomson, a director and company secretary, was due to a business transfer, since he was employed in the part of the undertaking which had been transferred. The Scottish EAT applying the ECJ's ruling in *Botzen*, where the ECJ ruled that if one part of a business is transferred the ARD only applies to the employees who are assigned to that part of the business being transferred, were able to conclude that Mr Thomson's presence in the part transferred meant he had rights, regardless of his employer's notice that he had been dismissed. Both these cases provide interesting judicial reasoning which suggests that UK judges could be intent on avoiding the ARD should they be given an opportunity to do so. However, recent guidance from the Court of Appeal in *ECM (Vehicle Delivery) Ltd* v. *Cox* (1998), to be discussed in detail in Chapter 6, suggests that where TUPE avoidance is observed then the courts will apply TUPE in such an event.

On the theme of a part transfer of a business the EAT in *Buchanan-Smith* v. *Schleicher & Co. International Ltd* (1996) considered the issue of the transfer of employees who were not solely working in the entity transferred. Mrs Buchanan-Smith was a director of the company which sold spare parts and serviced equipment. However, the sales division was closed down and the servicing and parts departments were transferred to Schleicher. In the course of submissions to the EAT, Schleicher maintained that this transfer was only a sale of assets. This argument was rejected by the EAT and it was held that a business transfer could be established on the basis that the identity had been retained.

In the significant case of *Wilson* v. *St Helens Borough Council* (1996) 'old' wounds regarding the usage of compromise agreements were reopened. The facts of the case were that Wilson was one of a number of employees employed in a council-controlled care home which had been transferred from Lancashire County Council to St Helens Borough Council in a business transfer accompanied by a change in terms and conditions. There was no evidence that the new terms had been accepted by the employees. The ET found that employees should not and did not sign away their rights and the EAT held that employers could buy out rights of employees, as they could dismiss and re-engage employees on new terms, since no detrimental change had occurred because TUPE had preserved the employees' rights. As Mummery J succinctly put it:

> It is true that there may be cases where an effective variation of the terms of employment does take place subsequently either by express agreement or by agreement inferred from conduct...[but] the law, surprising though it may be to English legal tradition, is clear. If the operative reason for the variation is the transfer of the undertaking, then the variation will be invalid.

However, on appeal, in the joined cases of *Wilson* and *Meade* (1996), the Court of Appeal allowing the appeal held that the existence of a business transfer itself did not justify a dismissal, unless the dismissal was for economic, organisational or technical reasons, as prescribed for in Regulation 8 of the TUPE Regulations. For *Wilson*, this meant that for an ET to find a variation in terms and conditions justifiable after a business transfer ETO reasons would have to be found, not solely that a transfer had taken place. Without these ETO reasons, any variation to terms and conditions became ineffective. In *Meade*, the outcome of the appeal meant that an agreement to employment by a former employee of the transferor with the transferee on 'new' terms and conditions was ineffective, albeit that an unfair dismissal claim could be founded. Thus the EAT had wrongly concluded that a dismissal notice was sufficient to terminate a contract. Clearly, these cases show that applying the *Daddy's Dance Hall* (1988) ruling, where it was held that 'an employee cannot waive the rights conferred upon him by the mandatory provisions of the Acquired Rights Directive 77/187 even if the disadvantages resulting from his waiver are offset from such benefits that, taking the matter as a whole, he is not placed in a worse position', can be overturned in some circumstances, but not in others. So, where does the law now stand on the variation of terms and conditions after a business transfer? That is surely a salient question to be addressed now by the House of Lords. Hopefully at last some clarification on the ETO reasons might be given (see Chapter 6).

In the Court of Appeal's judgment in *Betts*, Kennedy LJ noted that *Suzen* had created a 'shift of emphasis'. However, what I would reiterate from the thesis, in the context of these cases, is that the law now makes three salient points:

- In terms of identifying a business transfer, there is now a difference between first and second generation contracting out.

- A distinction can now be made (despite Kennedy LJ's *obiter* in *Betts*), if the facts suggest that it is justifiable, to distinguish between labour intensive and other business transfers.

- Scott-Baker J's clarity has now been destroyed and legal confusion abounds once more for contractors and employees alike subjected to business transfers.

Furthermore, the *Betts* case shows that *Dines* is the focal case. In my view, as Christopher Carr QC advocated in the *Betts* case, 'absurd results' most certainly do result when the CCT conflicts with the law relating to business transfers. Lastly, as the thesis contends, it is most bizarre that one German reference in *Suzen* should fly in the face of another German case, *Schmidt*. Clearly the ARD and TUPE have become exploited legal instruments which have been held together in part by ECJ rulings and clarified or undermined by some of the decisions delivered by the UK's EAT and Court of Appeal.

This growing UK common law on TUPE following ECJ rulings should allow both transferor and transferee alike to know whether there is going to be a business transfer without having to await the outcome of litigation. Clearly, Scott Baker J's appeal for clarity in the *Betts* case at first instance, referred to at the outset, has not been answered. In fact, the Court of Appeal, by applying *Suzen* in *Betts*, has added to legal confusion surrounding TUPE and the ARD. Moreover, the legal conflict between the outcomes delivered by the Court of Appeal in both *Dines* and *Betts* has now made it imperative that the House of Lords, which has not ruled on the ARD since *Litster* in 1989, be asked in some later case to resolve this conflict. Alternatively, what is clear from all this case law is that the legal framework governing business transfers is presently in a state of flux and needs reforming, the obvious long-term solution to this uncertainty and confusion surrounding business transfers being to revise the ARD.

Revising the ARD?

Following over forty rulings from the ECJ on the ARD, the EU Council agreed in 1998 to amend the Directive, after four years from

1994 to 1998 of political and legal wranglings among the EU institutions. The House of Lords Select Committee on the European Communities, Sub-Committee 'E' on 'EU Law and Institutions', in March 1996 published its Report on the EU Commission's proposed revised text. After hearing evidence from academics, representatives from both the unions and business, legal practitioners and others, it emerged that the main areas of controversy related to the scope of the ARD; the inclusions of share transfers, pensions, sea-going vessels and insolvency situations; the mandatory introduction of joint liability for a minimum of 12 months after the transfer; and the rights to information and consultation. Other matters which proved to be almost equally contentious concerned whether or not judicial authorities should be permitted to change terms and conditions and the setting of the threshold for applicability at the level of 50 employees. Two major concerns within the Committee were whether to maintain the exclusion of pension provision protection in the ARD and to reinforce the consultation rights, despite ECJ rulings on both these issues.

Professor Hepple in his written submission to the UK House of Lord's Committee outlined the general shortcomings of the existing 1977 directive, namely the unclear scope of the directive. In his evidence to the Committee, Professor Hepple suggested that the revised article 1 was 'wrong in principle' and did not achieve the clarity desired. As Lord Slynn later summarised the position in a debate on the report: 'Representatives of both employers and employees thought that this was not a helpful distinction to introduce between "activity" and "economic entity" particularly as it was thought that some activities could themselves constitute an economic entity' (See Hansard HL, 4 June 1996, col. 1192). CBI concerns centred upon the inclusion of contracting-out under the scope of the directive, which case law had already achieved. In seeking some moderation in this blanket application, the CBI submitted that '...the current situation damages contracting-out', resulting in delays in tendering, higher administrative costs and distorted competition. They also vehemently opposed the inclusion of pension rights under the directive. The TUC, while welcoming the EU Commission's attempts to clarify the law, were sceptical of its intentions should the proposed revisions seek to distort the ECJ's rulings. The TUC contended, like the ETUC, that the ARD provided a '...minimum floor of protection for workers in situations of business transfers' and consequently they did not want to see any proposed narrowing of the scope of the directive to exclude contracting-out or any other type of business transfers.

UK legal practitioners were represented by the Law Society and the Employment Lawyers Association. The Law Society advocated that the threshold of employees to which the ARD applied should be lowered to 20, in common with other recently enacted UK legislation such as the Disability Discrimination Act 1995, while the Employment Law Association (ELA) desired more differentiation between an economic entity and activity. They suggested that if the purpose of revised article 1(1) is to exclude such cases as *Schmidt*, then it had failed to do so. The ELA considered the implications of joint liability unfavourable, particularly in terms of equal pay, and were concerned that the inclusion of share transfers would alter the directive as it would no longer protect acquired rights but create 'new' ones.

The Society of Practitioners of Insolvency sought to highlight the distinction between the different objectives of bankruptcy law and employment law. Though they advocated greater clarity and were supportive of the rescue culture where business transfers were taking place due to liquidation, they recommended that TUPE should not apply to insolvent transfers. The argument in favour of the status quo was that an exclusion was based on the desire not to lower the number of potential rescuers of insolvent businesses due to the costs that would be incurred should they have to comply with the pre-existing terms and conditions. At this juncture, the Committee acknowledged the absence of any EU comparative evidence from other EU Member States with similar difficulties in this area. Other lobbyists included ACAS, the Business Services Association, CIPFA, the EOC, the LGIU, the LGMB and the RCN, among many others, each representing their respective interests. Meanwhile the UK government, represented by the Industrial Relations Division of the DTI, maintained that the application of the directive to contracting-out would restrict 'entrepreneurial freedom'. Thus this might inhibit, even distort, competition. The UK government also rejected any inclusion of liquidation proceedings, sea-going vessels and joint liability.

Historically, since *Litster* the British government has rejected the inclusion of liquidation proceedings on the grounds that its fears that including it under the ARD would cause many more insolvent undertakings not to be rescued. In the absence of evidence from the EU Commission the UK government chose to accept its own findings from its consultation process, with 93% opposed to it, and rejected the EU Commission's proposal on joint liability. While accepting that a sea-going vessel may be considered a physical asset of a business and therefore a potential transferable asset and thus within the remit of the ARD by some courts, the British government opted for the retention of the status quo and the EU's express exclusion of sea-going vessels under the Directive.

Having heard all of the evidence their Lordships Committee, consisting of both eminent practitioners, experts and academics, made the following main recommendations:

(i) To reject the Commission's proposed amendment to Article 1;

(ii) Share transfers should be included under the Directive;

(iii) Non-liquidation proceedings should be included under the Directive;

(iv) To reject the Commission's joint liability proposal;

(v) An EU definition of the term 'employee' should be provided for in the ARD;

(vi) To support the proposed changes bringing the text of Article 6 into line with the equivalent provisions of the Collective Redundancies Directive. But that the 50 employees threshold should be lowered to 20;

(vii) Agrees to extend the scope of the Directive to include sea-going vessels;

(viii) The Commission should consider the inclusion of 'comparable' pension rights.

The Committee also recommended that further clarity was required in respect of Articles 2(2), 4(1) and 4(5). In particular, their

Lordships advocated greater clarity on the criteria required to identify a 'stable economic entity'. Following from these comments and the concerns raised by the European Parliament, the EU Council received a final revised version of the Amended ARD in 1998 at the Cardiff Summit, to be discussed in detail in Chapter 7.

Summary

This chapter has set out the laws, both EU and domestic, governing business transfers. It has also summarised the key cases (the most recent developments are to be considered in Chapter 6), as well as highlighted the legal pitfalls and the case for clarity/reform of the regulatory framework.

To sum up, a 'relevant transfer' is a change in ownership of a business, or part of a business, where a transfer of significant assets or the taking over of a major part of a workforce occurs. Case law has provided guidance on 'what is a transfer' including the degree of similarity, the retention of identity, the transfer of physical and intangible assets, the transfer of staff, the cessation of activities, or the transfer of an 'economic entity' and/or an 'organised grouping with common tasks'. Where a transfer exists, what transfers are the existing contracts/contractual terms, liability for past breaches, all statutory liabilities, continuity of employment, personal injury liability, share options/profit shares/bonus schemes, the liability to inform and consult, collective agreements and TU recognition. What *does not* transfer are occupational pension rights (accrued pension rights are protected) and any criminal liabilities.

As observed ECJ milestone cases are:

- *Spijkers* – criteria for transfers (degree of similarity);

- *Rask* – retention of identity test;

- *Schmidt* – identify tangible/intangible assets;

- *Rygaard* – single 'economic entity';

- *Merckx* – contractual relationship transfers;

- *Henke* – excludes labour-intensive transfers;

- *Suzen* – economic entities test (excludes activities/ labour intensive transfers).

In a UK context, case law pre-TUPE includes:

- *Nokes* – dismissal/end of contract (no transfer);

- *Spence* – no liability transfers to transferee.

Post-TUPE case law includes:

- *Litster* – liabilities from transferor to transferee;

- *Dines* – identify identity and reasons (transferor's reasons);

- *Betts* – substantial labour transfers;

- *Wilson* – no changes to contracts post-transfer.

The most important ruling is the *Suzen* case where it was decided that ARD/TUPE does not apply where there is no transfer of staff, that service(s) transfers have no 'entity', and that a stable economic entity is required for the application of ARD/TUPE.

In the next chapter we examine the salient HR issues in business transfers and consider practical points arising from this complex legal framework.

CHAPTER 3

HR issues on business transfers

In every HR/business manager's mind is the implication of the increased maximum compensatory award for unfair dismissal (now £51,600) and the award of 13 weeks' pay per affected employee for failure to consult on business transfers. With such legal sanctions in mind, in this chapter we examine how TUPE operates in the business environment, its cost creation and liabilities. Evidently, it is paramount that those involved in business transfers identify such liabilities, apportion them and calculate their costs before transfer. Therefore, we will consider the process behind the sale of a business, the usage of warranties, indemnities and conditions, and 'due diligence'.

The 'transfer process'

A business transfer is in effect the sale of a business. As noted in the last chapter, in any business transfer under TUPE there are three distinct stages:

- information exchange and identification of legal and HR issues relating to the acquisition;

- drafting and negotiating the sale;

- concluding the sale (the contract for sale).

To shift liabilities in the transfer process, warranties and indemnities can be used:

- a *warranty* is a statement of fact on which the buyer relies in acquiring the business;

- an *indemnity* is an agreement between the parties allocating the cost to one party in a particular set of circumstances.

Exchanging information and 'due diligence'

It is important that each party to the business transfer acquires as much information as is possible before a contract is drafted. This step in the process is particularly important to the purchaser. Here time is a significant factor. To assist this process, a 'due diligence' questionnaire is used. Its aim is to set out a number of questions, clearly guided by TUPE principles, to which specific answers/details are provided by the seller(s) of the business. For example, the first essential 'due diligence' question is to ask: 'Who is the employer?' (i.e. the need to establish whether the business being acquired is the employer of the staff or whether a service company is operating). Clearly, from the example, if a service provider is *in situ*, then the purchaser will have to decide whether it will require staff to be transferred before the transfer or not, or even afterwards.

Below some basic 'due diligence' questions are set out:

- *Who is the employer?* This is to ascertain staff liability.

- *Who is being (will be) transferred?* This is to identify who is assigned to the part of the business which will transfer, or even who is employed in the undertaking affected. Also, these questions ascertain who is on sick leave, maternity leave, secondment or even a career break.

- *Has there been any consultation?* That is, have any employees been informed by the seller?

- *Have any employees objected to the transfer?* This is to clarify resignation implications.

- *Have there been any dismissals?* This is to ascertain whether any dismissals have occurred pre-transfer, in advance. Some vendors dismiss certain employees pre-transfer in order to make the business more attractive to prospective buyers, for instance so that labour costs are reduced. The latter may be the case where receivers or liquidators are involved. (It is also important to note here that an Employment Tribunal will focus upon the reasons for the dismissal rather than the timing of such. However, inferences in relation to connection with the transfer, past or pending, may be drawn in certain circumstances.)

- *What is the total number of transferable employees?*

- *What are the existing employment terms?* (A purchaser should seek disclosure of key information on directors and each employee – name, address, gender, race, age, job title and function, grade/scale (if applicable), continuous employment, pay scales.

Due diligence is therefore central to the information-gathering stage in the transfer of a business. In particular, discovering the exact terms and condition of each employee is crucial to the future success of both the business and the transfer process.

Examining employment terms

Before purchasing a business, an HR practitioner, lawyer or business manager ought to request copies of standard contracts of employment used by the transferor, and/or details of each employee's terms and conditions (including pay, review dates, future increments/increases, pay dates). Also, details regarding place(s) of work, notice period and any restrictive covenants should be sought. In particular, the existence of any restrictive covenants should be carefully examined (with the advice of lawyers), as such might prevent future business growth.

Restrictive covenants are transferred under TUPE. This means that the purchaser will be able to enforce them against the transferred workers. The issuance of new restrictive covenants to replace them should be avoided, as was the guidance given in the *Credit Suisse First Boston* v. *Litster* case (1998). The Court of Appeal held that the employee could not waive his TUPE protection as granted by the newly proposed restrictive covenant being imposed by the company in exchange for shares to the value of £600.

While the above examination is a good starting point for discovery, each business or business area (e.g. financial services, manufacturing) may have its own customs and practices with which you may or may not be familiar. In any case, you should check before purchase. In addition, you should request the following:

- copies of non-standard contracts of employment (including any service contracts);

- copies/details of arrangements for contract staff/agency staff (including consultancy agreements);

- copies of employment handbooks, other relevant policies, especially maternity, parental leave, equal opportunities, smoking, health and others);

- details of any benefits not specified in writing but agreed, such as enhanced redundancy scheme, sports/social benefits;

- details of any private health schemes, life assurance;

- details of pensions and pension schemes (including deeds of scheme and/or rules), shares, bonuses, profit-sharing;

- details of any compensation owed to any former employees (including directors);

- details of all existing HR/personnel policies and procedures, including disciplinary/grievance;

- details of any dismissals within a previous six-year period, including redundancies and consultation arrangements;

- copies of company accounts and tax returns, latest actuarial valuations;

- details of occupational health records;

- copies of health and safety policies (in particular, procedures and action lists, e.g. risk assessments and accident books, machinery and plant records, maintenance and safety inspections);

- details of any trade union recognition and/or membership information (including existing arrangements with trade unions, employee representatives, works councils and collective bargaining, including copies of any collective agreements;

- details of any past or threatened industrial conflict or strikes;

- details of any investigations by the EOC, CRE, DRC or HSE;

- details of legislation compliance, e.g. Working Time Regulations 1998, National Minimum Wage Act 1998, Data Protection Act 1998, Part-Time Workers Regulations 2000;

- details of any cases subject to the Public Interest Disclosure Act 1998, i.e. 'whistleblowing';

- details of any disputes with the Inland Revenue and/or Contributions Agency;

- details of current insurance, vicarious liability, personal injuries/accidents, etc. (especially those that may pre-date the transfer).

As explained in Chapter 2, since liabilities for some of these transfer on the sale of the business, it is prudent, if not diligent, to gather all the requisite information before drafting a contract for sale. Note that since occupational pension schemes do *not* transfer (albeit that equivalent pensions may be provided) nor do share option arrangements, it may be worth requesting details of any benefits which do *not* transfer, such as these pension schemes and benefits, for the sake of clarity and completion.

Under the principles of 'due diligence', the seller will respond to each question put by way of a 'disclosure letter'. Often where large numbers of papers are requested the vendor will set up a room at the business or elsewhere and allow the prospective purchaser to view the documents. Of importance is agreement by the vendor to update any information up to the date of transfer. Evidently, such information can determine purchase price, as well as what warranties and indemnities will be required from the vendor.

Once all disclosure has been satisfied, it is for the purchaser to review the information carefully and seek further details before reaching the draft contract stage.

Negotiating business transfers

Under TUPE, before negotiation for the sale of business commences, since the purchaser acquires liabilities as noted above, it is important that the buyer obtains all the relevant information needed to embark upon a negotiation. While TUPE facilitates the sale and transfers the employees, preserving their existing employment terms, it is common for the parties to negotiate the apportionment of liabilities.

The latter is done by way of indemnities (i.e. one party will indemnify the other for any of the liabilities for which the other would normally be liable under TUPE).

The following should be initially agreed:

- firstly, if TUPE applies, the parties should acknowledge the 'belief that TUPE applies';

- a date and time from when the transfer is to take effect should be settled;

- a list of the employees to be transferred should be agreed;

- an agreement on the apportionment of the employees' salary costs at time of transfer should be settled.

Following on from these basic agreements, the seller should set out his obligations ('that he will continue to perform his contractual obligations up to the transfer and will not vary or terminate contracts of employment before the business transfer takes place'). Further, the seller should make a statement informing the workforce that at the transfer, all employment information concerning employees will be passed to the purchaser (this is particularly important with reference to personnel files and data protection issues such as access to this information). Legally, the seller should also confirm compliance with Regulation 10 of TUPE, agreeing to consult and inform the relevant recognised trade unions or employee representatives.

From the purchaser's perspective, a statement should be made to the workforce, guaranteeing the obligations of meeting costs and liabilities arising at the transfer. However, the seller may also wish to include alternative provisions in case TUPE does not apply (such as requiring the purchaser to make comparable offers of employment, comparable pensions and indemnifying against costs arising out of failure to complete the contract).

Warranties and indemnities

Throughout the negotiation process, the usage of warranties and indemnities is crucial. Warranties can either be seeking a specific answer to a question or generally seeking assurances. Where definite warranties cannot be given, the words 'true to the best of knowledge and belief' should be used. Above all the purchaser should request the vendor to disclose information completely and accurately. This emphasises the important role played by the vendor's disclosure letter. Where warranties are included, this means that a purchaser can bring a claim for breach of warranty, normally up to an agreed maximum figure. Separate limits may be set for employment terms. Indemnities provide contractual obligations against the indemnifier who agrees to make payment to the other party with regard to any liabilities that arise, as agreed. For this reason, purchasers prefer indemnities to a decrease in the purchase price. Often assurances sought include that the provisions of TUPE will be adhered to. Below are some common indemnities and warranties.

Indemnities

In TUPE cases, indemnities are used to safeguard the purchaser from liabilities arising from the transfer, in particular the transferring employees. Basic indemnities cover the requirement of the vendor to indemnify the purchaser in respect of all pre-transfer liabilities (e.g. dismissals and discrimination claims). Alternatively, indemnities may cover post-transfer liabilities, especially in terms of litigation. Other indemnities include that the vendor discharges all obligations up to the transfer, covers unaccounted for employees, failure to provide relevant or accurate information, etc. Given the nature of these indemnities, the purchaser will often require a 'comfort letter', i.e. a guarantee of funds available to meet any breach of indemnity. Often such guarantees can be given by way of deposit of monies sufficient to cover the contingency. These deposits are usually held by solicitors acting for the contracting parties. Notwithstanding this usual practice, indemnities can be capped at a certain limit. As will be discussed in Chapter 7, the new Amended Directive of 1998 provides for Member States to make the transferor and transferee (contracting parties) to be jointly or severally liable, thus replacing the need for warranties, although it is unlikely that the UK government would impose such a provision in the near future.

Warranties

The warranties sought are derived from the seller's disclosure letter. Examples of common warranties include: that accurate particulars of employees' terms and conditions have been given; that the seller has disclosed an accurate sample of contracts of employment and handbooks and other supporting documentation; that the seller has not offered nor agreed any future variations to terms and conditions; and that the vendor does not employ any other persons than those listed in the 'transferring employees' document. Clearly, all warranties can be related to the 'due diligence' questionnaire discussed above.

Contract for sale of the business

The sale (i.e. the transfer) of the business is often conditional upon certain conditions, the so-called warranties and indemnities, being met. Whatever indemnities or warranties are included in the sale and purchase agreement will largely depend upon the bargaining positions of the parties in the negotiation. Once a contract is agreed and a date set for the transfer the sale is complete. However, even with the various warranties and indemnities in place following an effective 'due diligence' exercise, for some businesses, the HR issues are not over.

Harmonisation of terms of employment?

Imagine the relief of all the contracting parties once the transfer date arrives. However, for the transferee new problems might emerge, such as harmonisation of terms. For instance, if you transfer a business into an existing similar business the whole aim being to extend your market, then the two former employee groups on merger may become aware of different terms and conditions of pay, for example. The ready-made HR solution would be harmonisation. However, changing terms post-TUPE would undermine the primary purpose of TUPE. As discussed previously, the *Wilson* case should be noted, where the House of Lords held that even if employees agree to new terms and conditions they can subsequently reject those terms and sue the new employer. The danger with harmonisation of terms therefore is that transfer-connected variations to terms and conditions can become ineffective. Alternatively, a transferee could dismiss the employees and offer re-engagement on new terms, although good reasons against unfair dismissal claims would have to be met.

If a purchaser needs to harmonise terms then they need to establish economic, technical or organisational reasons for entailing changes in the workforce (Regulation 8). Moreover, a lapse of sufficient time post-transfer would have to occur before making such changes. It is unclear what a sufficient amount of time would be in these circumstances, such as to distance these changes from being connected to the transfer (three or six months, or longer?). It would be good practice to obtain the consent of all the employees affected by the proposed changes in advance. Alternatively, any existing flexibility within the contract or an implied term should be utilised to achieve your goal. Lastly, the use of incentive payments is another example.

Summary

This chapter has set out the HR and legal processes which underlie how business transfers occur. It has noted the key HR issues and principles and the negotiating issues to be considered, especially the importance of the three stages of due diligence, warranties and indemnities, and the contract for sale.

To sum up, in practical terms, key transfer issues are the existing employment terms, information and consultation, non-transferring employees, trade union recognition, pensions, and any existing/ current/pending litigation liabilities. The common identifiable problems with transfers are the changing terms and conditions, objecting employees, harmonisation of terms and inaccurate information.

In order to minimise risk, the legal principle of due diligence assists in questioning who the employer is, what the terms and conditions are, what benefits exist and for which employees, what the pensions situation is and the claims records, what the procedures are for health and safety, and what collective arrangements exist. Furthermore, warranties and indemnities can be used in order to establish statements of fact or provide general or specific guarantees. The common form of these is the usage of disclosure letters, comfort letters and deposits.

As noted, employees can refuse to transfer. However, refusal merely results in termination of employment (dismissal by transferor). Notably, fear of transfer cannot support a claim of breach of an implied term (trust) by the current/former employer.

What should also be noted is that the Directive only guarantees accrued pension rights and that there is no duty to transfer existing pensions and continue them into the future, although new advice shows that 'comparable'/equivalent pension provision is likely beyond 2001.

With regard to changes to the terms of employment, new terms effectively mean the repudiation of the contract, and even consent to new terms may not necessarily be binding according to developments in case law.

Above all, dismissal is automatically unfair if it is connected with the transfer, and liability for pre-transfer dismissals transfers across to the new employer. In establishing a link with the transfer time alone is not decisive. Although dismissal to attract a sale is unfair, dismissal designed to cut costs and reduce losses is not connected to the transfer.

In the next chapter we examine the legal and HR interface between contracting-out and business transfers.

CHAPTER 4

Contracting-out and business transfers

Now that the legal framework concerning business transfers has been cast, we now consider the policy that constantly challenges the TUPE framework. In the previous chapters numerous references have been made to contracting-out. It is this policy that has complicated TUPE more. Until 1980 the legal regimes of the public and private sectors within the UK were distinctly different; since the advent of Compulsory Competitive Tendering (CCT) the legal regime has recast the public sector more closely in the private sector model. While 'CCT' was a commonplace term in 1996, it has subsequently been replaced with 'Best Value' (since 2 January 2000) and other models for the contracting of services.

This chapter seeks to introduce and explain contracting-out and its impact upon TUPE. The law relating to business transfers in the UK presents a new problem when applied to contracting-out, with regard to whether or not contracting-out exercises amount to a business transfer. The case law to be discussed will address this question. A crucial question for business transfers concerns the method of introducing employment protection where public services are now in the hands of private sector operators.

What is contracting-out?

The public sector in the UK is now subject to a regime of contracting out and market testing of various functions to external service providers. It should be noted that UK government policy has asserted that contracting-out in the public sector 'ensures that competition is both free and fair'. Contracting-out therefore seeks to increase the effectiveness of market forces, in bringing about improved quality and cost-effectiveness by means of direct and indirect competition.

In a global context, from 1960 to 1990 the largest growth in the public sector occurred within the EU, while it had been moderate in the US. Three factors were highlighted as important when considering the public sector in a global context: wages, flexibility and mobility. In the 'Preface' of the UK government's *Market Testing Guidance*, the then Secretary of State, William Waldegrave MP, asserted that:

> Market testing is helping to improve the quality and the cost-effectiveness of many activities…In promoting the extension of market testing and competitive tendering we are endeavouring to ensure that competition is both free and fair.
>
> (HM Government, 1992)

Market testing has many forms. Generally, market testing is the subjection of public services to the discipline of the market. The various forms of market testing include facilities management, management buy-out, formerly Compulsory Competitive Tendering (CCT) and now 'Best Value'. CCT was in the 1980s and 1990s the most common and widely-used form of market testing or, as it is more generally known, contracting-out. The bedrock of contracting-out is a belief in the merits of the free market. The rationale behind contracting-out is that the provision of services in the public sector lacks competitive pressures which ensure efficient provision. From the outset it is important to distinguish contracting-out from privatisation. Privatisation concerns the situation where the assets involved in a service are directly transferred to private ownership. In contrast, contracting-out concerns the ideal of cost reduction in the provision of services in the public sector. Contracting-out is a process by which contractors compete with each other in an attempt to be awarded a particular contract.

Whether contracting-out is adopted or not, contractor failure remains another common feature of UK service provision, whether public or private. Contractor failure can be defined as a situation where a contractor fails to attain the service delivery standard previously agreed. Often the contractors become bankrupt and the service is not provided. One potential solution to this problem is the usage of performance bonds. Performance bonds are guarantees which safeguard against contractor failure. These bonds, or indemnities as they are commonly termed in law, are given so that if the contractor fails to attain the service standard agreed then the bond can be used to finance the ensuing retendering exercise. The so-called 'contractor specification' in the tendering process which translates the policy decision into service requirements by setting overall service objectives establishes the importance of such indemnities. This specification ensures that when bids are submitted they include performance bonds guaranteeing agreed quality levels of service delivery.

Contracting-out and TUPE

From 1979 onwards, the UK government introduced CCT in the public sector in order to increase efficiency and derive better value for money from service providers. Sceptical trade unionists believed that it was really an attempt to drive down wages and weaken employment rights in the public sector. In general employment law terms, contracting-out contributed to the disintegration of both traditional patterns of labour and business organisations themselves.

After nearly twenty years of legal wranglings before the ECJ on the scope of the TUPE Regulations, as discussed in Chapter 2, the UK government's established general guidance on contracting-out issued on 11 March 1993 advised contractors to evade TUPE by widely and creatively utilising the economic, technical or organisational (ETO) defences, contained in Article 4 of the ARD and Regulation 8 of TUPE. In particular, para. 9 of the UK government's guidance advises that within TUPE lies opt-out criteria from the protection granted by the ARD. All of these ETO defences are justifiable reasons for reducing labour costs and the workforce generally, either before or after a business transfer, whether instigated by CCT or not. The promotion of the wide usage of these defences displays the UK government's defiance of the *Rask* decision, already discussed in Chapter 2, which allowed employees subjected to contracting-out to be protected by the ARD (in the UK, TUPE).

It is stated that avoidance of TUPE gives cost benefits. Many contractors continue to argue that if TUPE applies then they would not be able to compete with either the direct service organisation (DSO)/in-house provider (the in-house, existing service providers who executed the service prior to the contracting-out regime) or the current service provider (the competitor). This is an argument which the UK government preserved in its CCT policy and thus, simultaneously, in its approach towards TUPE and the ARD. Hence, it could be argued that any business transfers under contracting-out could potentially be justified on ETO grounds. These ETO defences therefore could undermine the TUPE Regulations while increasing efficiency and competitiveness.

Since the Conservative's 1992 Election Manifesto, which made specific reference to 'bringing the private-sector enterprise into the public services', CCT has been implemented in many areas of both central and local government activities. The 1980 and 1988 Local Government Acts, as well as the NHS and Community Care Act 1990, the Civil Service (Management Functions) Act 1992, the Criminal Justice and Public Order Act 1994 and the Deregulation and Contracting Out Act 1994, which included the Prison Education Service, heralded the restructuring of the UK public sector. Contracting-out has involved restructuring in both the blue and white collar services previously provided by local authorities, the health service and central government. Following a test run with building services under the Local Government Planning and Land Act 1980, the Local Government Act 1988 introduced CCT to refuse collection, cleaning, catering and leisure facilities as the next areas to be exposed to market forces.

A tendering process lies at the heart of all of these statutory schemes. They all commence with a service provider, for example a local authority or hospital, putting out a particular service to tender. The local authority/council or health authority becomes known thereafter as the 'client side'. The tendering process begins with a 'contract specification', already alluded to, being drafted, followed by the publication and circulation of a notice of intention to tender in the press. As noted in Chapter 3, before the specification is concluded, some consideration should be afforded to staffing issues. In particular this guidance stated that it would be regarded as anti-competitive to specify a service to apply the Transfer of Undertakings Protection Regulations (TUPE) to staff. The process continues with the tenderers replying to the advertisements by submitting a tender document, commonly referred to solely as a 'tender', within 37 days. A 'tender' has to be made in writing and be a signed statement making a bid and stating that the contractor, at this stage 'tenderer', will supply services for a given price. Following the submission of the bids, an evaluation of the bids takes place which is followed by an awarding of the contract. There is usually 120 days between the awarding of the contract and its commencement. Thereafter, the contractor is referred to as the 'service provider'. The evaluation process considers various factors, such as the costs of awarding the work to an external contractor, redundancy payments, matters relating to the tenderer's financial standing, geographical factors, the contractor's local knowledge and the tender price. A maximum of 90 days is set for tender evaluation. These tender documents substantiate a draft contract giving details of the contractor/service provider's practices as an employer. These will include information on grievance and disciplinary procedures, staff training, standards of service, staff uniforms, health and safety at work policies, and details about the re-employment of existing staff. Once the invitation to tender period closes, the existing service provider, strongly influenced by what is already being provided by in-house providers, selects a contractor.

Throughout this tendering process, the council/health authority, the original client-side service provider, is obliged to publish a notice of tender in a local newspaper eliciting applications to appear on a list of nominated contractors, issue a reasonable specification, send out invitations to tender, invite written bids from the direct service organisation (DSO)/in-house provider, ensure that fair competition between all bidders exists, and explain their decision in favour of a particular bidder. This transparent tendering process ensures that information is given to all parties concerned and thus lowers the prospect of uncertainty and misunderstanding between the parties concerned, thereby reducing the risk of contractor failure. In any event, should such communication break down, then aggrieved tenderers can complain to the DETR whereupon the Minister could award the contract if it deems the client-side, the original service provider, to have acted out of its obligations, by issuing a section 13 Order.

Ordinary business transfers vs. contracting-out transfers

Such an expansive statutory framework rooted in competition and best value policy has affected TUPE. In practical terms, it emerges that two categories of transfer arise: ordinary or contracting-out. In order to distinguish the two categories, contracting-out (or contracting-in) prevails in three situations: an organisation contracts out a contract for goods or services for the first time (first generation); or the first contractor is replaced by a second, third, fourth, etc. contractor (second generation); or, the client takes the contracted-out activities back in-house (contracting-in). All other situations are ordinary sales of businesses (hence ordinary business transfers). Note it is only under contracting scenarios that TUPE can frustrate the vendor/seller and purchaser's commercial intentions. TUPE will not apply if the contract is won on a contracting-out basis by an in-house team because there is no change of employer.

Practical issues on TUPE with contracting-out

Irrespective of whether the business transfer results from a contracting-out exercise or not, it is vital for the both the vendor and purchaser to give full consideration to TUPE issues. In particular, the stages, processes and principles set out in Chapter 3 observed how important the contractual issues were and this may be more important in the context of contracting-out transfers, since a major criticism of contracting-out has been that it establishes a multifarious tangle of contractual relationships rather than one single economic unit. Arguably, the creation of a network of separate contractor units allows for greater flexibility in the employment environment. This presents the first practical problem for TUPE: who is the employer and who are the employees (see points made in Chapter 3, in terms of contractual issues). Therefore, a due diligence exercise is very important in order to ascertain the rights and liabilities involved.

Secondly, if the contracting-out exercise is based on the assumption that TUPE does *not* apply and the bidders/purchaser believe that TUPE does not, then how are the parties to proceed given their knowledge of TUPE? Two options emerge: (a) revise the bid/purchase to take account of TUPE; or (b) proceed as agreed taking account of all the legal and HR risks that are involved. Such a situation could well test the limits of the due diligence test.

Within the context of contracting-out transfers, the final written agreement for sale may include the sale of assets, both tangible and intangible (such as goodwill) and the transfer of employees. Consequently, such an agreement may either contract in or out the services. To that end, the parties should specify which it is for the sake of clarity in terms of the application of TUPE. Can TUPE ever be evaded? TUPE is not there to be evaded and the courts must prevent this from occurring. Regulation 12 of TUPE provides that 'Any provision of any agreement...shall be void in so far as it purports to exclude or limit the operation of Regulation 5, 8 or 10.' However, such wording can be avoided under a compromise agreement regulated by s. 203, ERA 1996 (the latter agreement being binding and valid), and the transferee (new employer) may refuse to take on the staff subject to transfer. The latter prevails as the weakest of the two options and likely to be questionable before the courts following the *ECM* v. *Cox* (1998) case to be discussed later in Chapter 6.

From reading Chapter 2 it emerges that the test as to whether TUPE applies in contracting-out situations is now recognised to be no different from the test as to whether TUPE applies in the context of an ordinary business transfer, since you need to identify a stable economic entity (i.e. identify the assets, be they production or employees). Next you need to consider what proportion of these assets will transfer. If it is significant, then TUPE automatically applies. Whether TUPE applies or not is a question of fact in each case, but the starting point for contracting-out should be to assume that TUPE applies.

More practical problems arise in second-generation contracting-out. This is simply because the first-generation (original) client and contractor will have set the standard having negotiated a contract (or service level agreement) with relevant warranties and indemnities. Clearly, there is limited scope for the second-round contractor since there is no contract between it and the outgoing contractor, and a limited scope for obtaining information exists. The remedy available for this is to stipulate in the first contract that the first contractor must indemnify subsequent contractors for the first contractor's acts or omissions, as well as providing information and documentation concerning its employees at the end of the contract period.

To ease practical problems in the public sector the UK government issued in 1991 a 'Statement of Practice' setting out the principles that should apply to the public sector. This specifies that all contracting-out should apply TUPE, including all second-generation exercises and even where in limited circumstances TUPE may not apply the TUPE principles should be adhered to, although this Statement only applies to the transfer of staff from the public sector to the private or voluntary sectors.

Pensions, as in ordinary transfer cases, are a further contentious issue in contracting-out. The practical problem that arises in terms of pensions in contracting-out situations is the disparate provision. The guiding principle should be that the new employer offers those staff affected membership of a 'broadly comparable' pension scheme.

Another practical problem presented by TUPE to contracting-out situations is that public sector trade union recognition is more common than in the private sector. A private sector contractor may then find itself dealing with a collective environment that it is unfamiliar with. Apart from the obvious solution of de-recognition, in light of the 1999 Employment Relations Act such a solution may be a difficulty given the procedural mechanics presented by this scheme. A related issue is that of consultation: where no previous experience of unions/employee representatives exists, then the need to create consultation arrangements is necessary (as will be discussed in the next chapter, Chapter 5).

The final practical problem is that of equal pay and is particularly pertinent to the public sector. Notably the Equal Pay Act 1970 provides that the claimant must show a comparator, broadly undertaking the same or like work, employed on common terms and conditions. While job evaluation schemes are common in the public sector, North Yorkshire County Council paid out £4 million to employees having been dismissed and re-employed on a lower rate of pay in order to reduce costs. The House of Lords held that the need to cut costs was not a material factor and therefore not a defence.

Contracting-out, TUPE and the law

In Chapter 2 of this book the legal framework which surrounds business transfers was discussed. We will now examine how the law specifically manages business transfers under contracting-out exercises. As we are by now aware the UK court's inability to recognise a functional identity of an ancillary activity has caused much of the confusion surrounding the legal regulation of business transfers. English law's recognition of the existence of contracting out was first noted in the *Rastill* decision in 1978. Since then, three important decisions of the ECJ with regard to contracting-out, notably *Rask*, *Schmidt* and *Rygaard*, have arisen. At a domestic level, many attempts have been made to evade the obligations under TUPE, especially by those in pursuit of contracting-out. A contractor's primary aim is to seek out lower unit labour costs, and this objective has confronted the TUPE's primary aim to protect employees' rights subjected to transfers, although the ARD's (that of TUPE in the UK) aim is being upheld at the EU level, for example in the *Rask* and *Schmidt* decisions, previously discussed, where the ECJ held that such contracting-out was protected under the directive and that the ARD explicitly applied to contracting-out.

In the UK, the *Dines* case introduced in Chapter 1 highlights that contracting-out will not be allowed to impede the worker's protection afforded by TUPE. The central well-rehearsed question in this case was whether there was an identifiable economic entity and whether it had been disposed of as a going concern. In order to answer this question, applying the ECJ's rulings in the *Spijkers* and *Rask* cases, already discussed in Chapter 2, and the UK Court of Appeal's judgment in *Dines*, enables the enquirer to establish whether there is a business transfer by deciding whether the business retains its identity or not.

The decision of the House of Lords in *Ratcliffe* v. *North Yorkshire County Council* (1995) involving the contracting-out of the provision of school meals under the Local Government Act 1988, recognised that CCT threatened the status quo in working conditions and employment protection. The complexity surrounding this misconceived equal pay claim arose with regard to whether an employer can rely upon external market forces as a defence for discriminatory changes in the rates of pay. The Court of Appeal concluded that the market forces defence was a reasonable justification. The Court of Appeal held that the operation of contracting-out does amount to a transfer and that the UK's Regulations were in breach of the EU's directive on transfers. The ET had misdirected itself in holding that when there is a change of contractors, there is a cessation of the business and that business transfers may take place in two or more phases. The House of Lords, overturning the Court of Appeal's ruling, dismissed the economic defence presented as a genuine material factor, permissible in equal pay cases in certain circumstances, similar to the ETO for business transfers.

Lord Slynn's leading speech revitalised hope anew for those subject to contracting-out transfers by placing economics second to employee's rights. Following *Dines* and *Schmidt*, an acceptance of

CCT under the scope of the ARD could now provoke a wider usage of the ETO defences, particularly since CCT is an example of market forces at work. And so it can be intimated that a CCT transfer inherently gives rise to an automatic ETO defence. We will return to this growing important issue in the next section of this chapter.

Nevertheless, other decisions of the UK courts prior to *Dines* have shown other procedural ways and means of complaining about dismissals in connection with transfers. Two important domestic decisions, *Kenny* (1993) and *Porter* (1993), demonstrate that action against dismissal by way of business transfer can alternatively be initiated in the High Court. For example, *Kenny*, a case involving lecturers at Her Majesty's Youth Custody Centre (HMYCC) Thorn Cross who underwent a CCT exercise and a subsequent business transfer, held that a legal business transfer had occurred since the business transferred had retained its identity.

In the *Porter* case, the plaintiffs seeking a declaration were employees of Trent Regional Health Authority, employed as consultant paediatricians at Kesteven General Hospital. Following the conviction of Beverly Allitt, a former paediatric nurse at Kesteven General Hospital, after an enquiry into the deaths of babies, the Trent Regional Health Authority terminated their arrangements with the Kesteven Hospital and entered into a contract with another NHS trust for the provision of paediatric services. The 'new' contractor created four consultant paediatric posts to service the contract. However, the Regional Health Authority asked the NHS trust contractor to re-engage all staff, including the plaintiffs. They did warn Porter and others that it might lead to the posts becoming redundant. On 25 March the

Regional Health Authority sent Porter et al. formal notices of their redundancy. On 30 April, Porter and others were interviewed for the vacant posts, but were unsuccessful.

Subsequently, Porter sought a declaration under Order 14A that their contracts of employment took effect as originally made with the defendants rather than the Regional Health Authority. Porter contended that the reorganisation fell within the ARD, since an undertaking had been transferred. Furthermore, the Regional Health Authority disputed that there had been any termination of the contract and that the ARD did not apply in the instant case. They conceded that TUPE did not give full effect to the ARD which was directly enforceable against a public body, such as an NHS trust. The High Court held that Order 14A was appropriate where the plaintiffs, Porter et al., could establish facts which showed that the conclusion must be that there was a business transfer, the court's reasoning being that a 'relevant' business transfer, despite s. 4(3), NHS and Community Care Act 1990 which does not deprive an NHS contract of its legal effect, was effected. A business transfer was established under Article 1(1) of the ARD and following the ECJ's pronouncement in *Redmond*, where a change in the provider of such services brought about a business transfer as the responsibilities of the Regional Health Authority remained unchanged.

It remains a growing anxiety among lawyers that the legal pronouncements on contracting-out could merely be the tip of the iceberg, since a further problem may be encountered in the not too distant future. For instance, the EAT upheld that contracting-in amounted to a transfer in *Betts* v. *Brintel Helicopters Ltd* (1996). 'Contracting-in' is a term used to define a situation where the originally defeated service provider retenders and resumes the service provision which they undertook before the first contracting-out exercise took place. The facts of the case were that the Isles of Scilly Council owned and managed St Mary's Airport until 1986, when they decided to seek tenders for the management contract. Subsequently, Brintel Helicopters became the service provider. The contract was terminated on 1 January 1993 and all employees concerned were made redundant. After the event they were re-employed by the council on less favourable terms and conditions. An ET upheld the employees' complaints, since there was a sufficient 'economic' entity. The council appealed to the EAT on the ground that there was no business transfer. Adopting a purposive approach and the Court of Appeal's guidance in the *Dines* decision, the EAT dismissed the appeal having established a transferable 'economic entity', by rejecting the contention that a 'labour-only business' prevented a business transfer from occurring. The Court of Appeal decision in *Betts* has already been discussed in Chapter 2.

In terms of further clarification, the Scottish EAT in the *Kelman* (1995) case applied *Dines*, the EAT's decision in *Brintel* and the ECJ's ruling in *Schmidt*, to hold that a business transfer had occurred since the identity of the undertaking had survived the business transfer. *Kelman* was another case involving a CCT exercise under the Local Government Act 1988. Following the tendering exercise, Grampian Direct Services Organisation (GDSO) took charge of the provision of school cleaning from 1 January 1989. From 1989 to 1992, the cleaners experienced no change. The GDSO was not as successful in the retendering exercise in 1992, obtaining only four out of the five contracts. Consequently, the fifth area was awarded to Care Contract Services Ltd and Phyliss Kelman and others were made redundant. She had been a supervisor earning £4.04 an hour but was offered only £3.38 an hour by the 'new' service provider. Mrs Kelman complained to an ET. The ET found no 'TUPE transfer', although the EAT with the benefit of the ECJ's recent ruling in *Schmidt* found to the contrary and upheld Mrs Kelman's claim. This decision, to some degree, clarifies the law, which is much welcomed.

Returning briefly to the issue of contracting-out and discrimination, the EAT in the *DJM International Ltd* v. *Nicholas* (1996) case held that liability for sex discrimination could be transferred following a business transfer. Despite the fact that the alleged act of discrimination concerned took place prior to the business transfer under a previous contract of employment, once the business is transferred the liability for that discrimination also becomes transferable. In the words of the President of the EAT, Mummery J:

> ...a liability may be incurred by an employer to an employee and that subsequent change in the contractual relationship between the employer and employee does not prevent that liability from transferring to the transferee of the undertaking.

The House of Lords' decision in the *Ratcliffe* case goes some way to confirm the potential of such a claim by the EOC. This is to be discussed later. Similarly the case of the former Cleveland County Council dinner ladies' claim for sex discrimination, when they were contracted out and lost their holiday pay during vacations while the male workers kept theirs, was deemed to be sex discrimination and resulted in out-of-tribunal awards of compensation.

Following these decisions, practitioners now find it increasingly difficult to advise where contracting-out, or any change of service provider, will not be covered by TUPE. In particular, the *Betts* decision poses a future problem when contracting-out comes to an end and the previous provider resumes control. Ostensibly, the growing UK common law surrounding the ARD and TUPE alike following ECJ rulings has either assisted in clarifying the law or mystifying the parties involved, the latter being due to the incremental nature of the ETO defences being used by contractors' lawyers. What is clear from all this case law is that the legal framework governing business transfers is presently in a state of flux and so adds weight to the arguments, already canvassed in this thesis, in favour of legal reform of the ARD. Clearly, the ARD and TUPE have been legal instruments solely held together by ECJ rulings and clarifications delivered by both the EAT and Court of Appeal. Much of the recent uncertainty surrounding business transfers has been presented by the UK's contracting-out policy.

The 'ETO' defences and contracting-out

In the preceding chapters of this book, one could rightly have drawn the conclusion that TUPE is a one-sided piece of legislation solely in favour of protecting worker's rights. As HR and legal practitioners alike know, that is not so since the ETO defences preserve the EU Commission's original intentions to create market harmonisation. Article 4(1) of the ARD expressly limits its application on dismissals subject to ETO reasons which the employer can give.

The ETO defences have attracted little attention from either the ECJ or the EU Commission. Following their Lordships' deliberations in the *Ratcliffe* case, discussed above, much of the debate surrounding business transfers has now moved towards the applicability of the ETO defences. Regulation 8 of TUPE provides three defences derived from Article 4 of the ARD, though Regulation 8(1) provides that 'where either before or after a relevant transfer, any employee of the transferor or transferee is dismissed, that employee shall be treated…as unfairly dismissed if the transfer or a reason connected with it is the reason or principal reason for his dismissal'. This automatic unfairness rule is linked to the 'escape route' provided for under Regulation 8(2) which states that 'where an economic, technical or organisational reason entailing changes in the workforce of either the transferor or the transferee before or after a relevant transfer, is the reason or principal reason for dismissing the employee'.

The EU passivity on these ETO defences might be explained by the opinions of Advocates-General in two leading ECJ rulings. For instance, Advocate-General Darmon in *Bork* suggested that the ETO defences were restricted where '…the undertaking's resumption of business was envisaged'. This declaration has led the ECJ to believe that the applicability of the ETO defences is narrow and most certainly inapplicable should the business continue post-transfer. Following this advice, the ECJ held that Article 4(1) of the ARD shall not in itself constitute grounds for dismissal and that the employees transferred were to be treated as still employed, albeit now by the transferee. Relying upon Darmon's comments in *Bork*, Advocate-General Van Gerven, some three years later, in *D'Urso* (1992), restated more vociferously that the ARD:

...expressly prohibits dismissals when they are the result of the transfer of the undertaking. Only dismissals which would have been made in any case, for instance if the decision was taken before there was any question of transferring the undertaking, fall within the exclusion. Article 4 cannot therefore be relied upon as a support for an argument for dismissing some of the employees because the undertaking has been transferred.

Van Gerven therefore concludes that the ETO defences cannot be relied upon as a justification for dismissals. However, the ECJ in *D'Urso*, while generally approving of the Advocate-General's advice, stated that although Article 4(1) of the ARD forbade '...the use of the transfer itself as a reason for dismissal...on the other hand, the Directive shall not stand in the way of dismissals which may take place for economic, technical or organisational reasons'. Such reasoning, this thesis will contend, will open the floodgates for the next wave of contracting-out business transfers litigation. The contradictory nature of the ECJ's approach to the ETO defences perhaps explains the ECJ's passivity on these ETO defences. This thesis will challenge the ECJ's passivity as, irrespective of these rulings, the debate surrounding the ARD, having moved on from the scope of the ARD, now lies in whether there is an ETO reason. The central issue here is what constitutes an 'ETO' defence? Although it is now clear when it should apply, when they are appropriate not only depends upon the facts, but on their definition. Both the ARD and the TUPE Regulations fail to define them and more recently EU legislators sought not to define them in their proposed revision of the ARD. The ECJ up to now has also not ruled on this issue.

Interestingly enough, the UK government sought to define these terms in its guidance issued in March 1993. William Waldegrave MP, then the Chancellor of the Duchy of Lancaster, defined 'economic' to mean 'where a demand for an employer's output has fallen that profitability could not be sustained'; stated that 'technical' referred to the usage of 'new technology and the employees did not have the necessary skills'; and described 'organisational' as a situation which arises 'where a new employer operates at a different location and it is not practical to relocate'. Overall, this exercise recognised that the UK courts had tended towards a narrow interpretation of such reasons, but that in such cases dismissal might be fair provided the employer had acted reasonably to allow an exclusion.

Previous cases have considered what is meant by the term 'economic'. For instance, in the Scottish EAT, the case of *Meikle* v. *McPhail (Charlston Arms)* (1983) held that the term connoted a commercial objective. This case concerned the transfer of a pub which was, in the opinion of the new employer and publican, overstaffed. Ostensibly, the new owner, the transferee, soon realised that unless he made a staff reduction, the business could not be run profitably. This argument lends support to the view that the purpose of the ETO defences are to remove the actual economic burdens from new employers when subjected to business transfers by sanctioning so-called 'economic dismissal'. No cases at present have addressed what is meant by the term 'technical'. However, it is assumed that this covers situations where an employee is dismissed because he or she does not have the necessary technical know-how or experience for the job which has changed for technological reasons, for example in the use of new equipment. This might include, in a contracting-out context, the usage of 'wheelie bins' replacing old static waste or refuse bins, or the usage of larger vehicles or different machinery.

The High Court has summarily adjudicated on what is meant by 'organisational' in the *Porter* (1993) case, as mentioned above. In the context of the ETO defence, the defendants contended that the redundancy notices issued to the appellants were issued for organisational reasons. This case being an example of where a public body decided to terminate its arrangement with one person and replace it with an arrangement with another having similar aims, a business reorganisation was also incurred. The defendants argued that it was for this reason that the plaintiffs were dismissed. The court stated, per Sir Godfray Le Quesne, that:

> I have no doubt that this amounted to a reorganisation of the services. It cannot be said that the reorganisation did not entail changes in the workforce because the defendants should have appointed the plaintiffs to the positions for which they had applied. The relevant change in the workforce, as I have said was in my view the termination of the existing contracts of the Plaintiffs. That is the change which was entailed by the organisational reasons.

The peculiar outcome of the *Porter* case throws the effectiveness of the legislation open to question, particularly when, despite the ARD's declared aim, the directive did also provide for these ETO justifications. The fact remains that although TUPE might apply, the ETO defences could rescue an employer from any liability. More than likely, the long-term effects of the *Porter* decision will be that the ETO defences might now be used by employers who undertake contracting-out business transfers, a situation which raises widespread concern among UK unions. Following *Porter*, applying Article 4(1) of the ARD, which provides that a business transfer 'shall not of itself constitute grounds for dismissal by the transferor or the transferee', to CCT business transfers means that the ETO justifications can indirectly prevail and any notices of termination served upon employees pre- or post-transfer will not be invalid at common law. Under the ARD, Article 3 provides for these rights to be carried post-transfer. Since there had been a valid termination, the plaintiffs were redundant. The court in dismissing the application addressed the central questions of whether there was a business transfer and whether this had been the result of a legal business transfer. Essentially, the High Court in *Porter* decided that the Regional Health Authority's decision to transfer its contract for the provision of paediatric services from one of its hospitals to an NHS trust was a business transfer covered by the ARD. Thus the contracts of employment of two consultants who had worked under the old contract would be transferred to the trust. The ARD did not prevent the termination of the consultant's contracts by allowing the trust to have a restricted choice in who to appoint to the consultants' posts in the new service on the grounds of an organisational defence.

The decision of the Employment Appeal Tribunal in the case of *BSG Property Services* v. *Tuck* (1996) and others has at last placed the ETO defences on the legal agenda. For a while now many HR and legal practitioners have awaited the debate surrounding business transfers to move on from the now well-trod path of how to identify 'a relevant transfer' and whether contracting-out is within the scope of the ARD, to what is meant in both the directive and the TUPE Regulations by the term 'ETO'. The facts of this case concern the Mid-Bedfordshire District Council Housing Maintenance Direct Service Organisation (DSO) which employed a team of 14 jobbers, including Mr Tuck, a carpenter, and other joiners, plumbers and bricklayers, until they decided to terminate their contract with the council on 12 February 1993. This litigation arose since three months later in May 1993 the council, following a retendering exercise, contracted with BSG Property Services to provide the housing maintenance formerly operated by the DSO. It was agreed between the council that the work carried out by Tuck and others was to be undertaken by self-employed tradesmen. Both the council and the 'new' contractor believed that TUPE did not apply, as they concluded that there was no transfer of undertaking. Subsequently, Tuck and others' employment with the DSO was terminated by the council on the grounds of redundancy. Tuck and others decided to claim unfair dismissal.

An ET found that a relevant transfer had occurred and that the dismissals were connected with the transfer, although the tribunal took the view that they were not unfairly dismissed. The ET also held that redundancy was the reason for the dismissal and that the fact that BSG did not engage any employees was due to economic or organisational reasons within Regulation 8(2)(b). The employees' claims therefore failed. On appeal, *Tuck* and others appealed against the finding of an ETO defence and BSG appealed on the grounds that the tribunal had established that a transfer had occurred.

The EAT held that the tribunal had not erred in holding that a transfer had taken place. Considering all the facts, the EAT established that the activities concerned constituted an 'undertaking' capable of being transferred. Applying the Court of Appeal's approach in *Dines* and the ECJ's ruling in the *Rygaard* case, Mummery J held that a 'stable economic entity' had been transferred. Considering all the relevant case law, the EAT reiterated that where an employee is dismissed by the transferor, even if it transpires after the transfer, it is the transferor who dismisses. Accordingly, the relevant reason for the dismissal is determined by the transferor, the council, despite liability for the dismissal connected with the transfer being passed to the transferee, BSG. It followed therefore that the council's reason for the dismissals was the relevant reason. Relying upon the former relevant statutory provisions, ss. 53, 54(1) and 55(2) of the EPCA 1978, and the principle enunciated in *Devis & Sons* v. *Atkins* (1977), the reason given by the council on the effective date of termination and in writing thereafter was the reason for the dismissal.

On the facts, the EAT agreed that the tribunal had incorrectly found that the council did have an ETO defence for the dismissals. The EAT ruled that because the council and BSG did not believe that TUPE applied then no ETO defences could arise in the instant case. TUPE admission, therefore, becomes a precondition for the ETO defences. In addition, BSG, in not believing that TUPE applied, did not consider themselves to be the transferee at all in any event, though, pursuant to Regulation 5, they were subject to all the liabilities of the council in connection with the contracts of employment. Had no transfer occurred, then the council would have remained liable. As for the transferee, although they did not conduct the dismissals, but as a result of a transfer became liable for them, then they were bound by the council's reason which did not give rise to an ETO defence. The interesting point which the EAT raises in its decision in this case is that no ETO reason can be relied upon unless TUPE applies. In Mummery J's words: 'They did not believe that they had to have such a reason, because they did not believe that the 1981 Regulations applied.' It could not be any clearer that a belief that TUPE does not apply means that no ETO defence could have been considered or arise as a reason for the transfer should one be established. In addition, the EAT confirmed that a transferee is bound by the transferor's reasons. It therefore remains clear law that Regulation 8's automatic unfairness rule applies to dismissals whether they are effected before or after the date of the business transfer, without any specific limitation in time.

Essentially, the EAT ruling produces a three-stage test when applicants or appellants alike seek to rely upon the ETO defences. Firstly, it must be established that an ETO reason was connected with the business transfer; secondly, an onus is on the employer to show that the principal reason falls within the scope of Regulation 8 which entails changes in the workforce; and lastly, the reasonableness of the decision must be assessed in all the circumstances. This threefold test requires a link between a dismissal and a business transfer, a test which confirms the *ratio decidendi* of the EAT ruling in *Wheeler* (1987), a case involving the transfer of a business where the prospective purchaser insisted upon the dismissal of all the existing staff. The EAT concluded that an 'economic' reason for dismissal to fall within Regulation 8(2) of the TUPE Regulations 1981 must be one which relates to the conduct of the business. The EAT in the *Wheeler* case provides some restraint on recalcitrant employers who undertake transfers and attempt to hide behind the ETO defences. It held that in order to shield your business by an ETO reason for the transfer requires the conduct of the business to give rise to such a defence. More recent ETO cases will be considered in Chapter 6.

The future of TUPE and contracting-out

Evidently, the ETO defences raise more specific questions in respect of contracting-out. That being so, does any contracting-out exercise inherently have an economic defence? If so, that might be met with further confusion among the judges, as already seen in non-contracting-out cases. For example, in *Trafford* v. *Sharpe* (1994), a case involving redundancies post-transfer, the EAT considered an 'ETO' defence. Adopting a purposive approach towards the construction of Regulation 8, Mummery J stated that:

> The rights of workers must be safeguarded 'so far as possible'. It is not always possible to safeguard the rights of workers. As is recognised…the rights of workers not to be dismissed on the transfer of an undertaking must not stand in the way of dismissals which take place for economic reasons entailing changes in the workforce. In such cases the rights of workers may be outweighed by the economic reasons.

However, whose economic reasons was Mummery J referring to? This decision presents ambiguity, in so far as it reinforces usage of the ETO defences. This judgment blatantly asserts that the ARD no longer safeguards the employee first and foremost. Instead the primary objective of the ARD is subject to a weighing up of the employer's economic situation against the employee's livelihood. Such a decision sends out a clear message to employers to evade the legislation.

This lies in stark contrast to the House of Lords' decision in the *Ratcliffe* case, previously discussed. Applying the House of Lord's ruling to business transfers, rather than the Equal Pay Act which the case concerned, such an evasion of the Regulations was exactly what the ARD was seeking to prevent. As we are already aware the ARD sought to safeguard employees. Lord Slynn, in giving the leading judgment, rejected the economic reason forwarded by the Council for the pay decreases incurred by their former employees post-transfer. In Lord Slynn's words: 'Though conscious of the difficult problem facing the employers in seeking to compete with a rival,…that…was the very kind of discrimination in relation to pay which the Act sought to remove.' While these cases concern solely the 'economic' aspect of the ETO defences, Scott J in the *Wheeler* case affirmed that '…the adjective, "economic", must be construed *ejusdem generis* with the adjectives "technical" and "organisational".' Applying such deliberations to CCT cases, the ETO defences might not be easily utilised. Although, where contracting-out business transfers exist, the fact that they are economically motivated may result in easier application of the ETO defences. Again, Scott J's guidance in *Wheeler* sheds some further light onto the issue, when the EAT suggested that any dismissals should be 'genuinely economic, technical or organisational'. The term 'genuinely' will either permit the extension of these defences or restrict them.

It would appear that the *Tuck* case pushes the future debate surrounding business transfers into a discussion about the applicability and substance of the much-quoted and, until now, little used 'ETO' defences. This decision of the EAT presents another problem for those concerned with business transfers. Following this decision, will contractors now accept that TUPE applies and agree on an ETO reason before transfers take place? The central question remains unanswered: how will the courts in the UK or the ECJ interpret these ETO defences? Perhaps upon reflection the former President of the EAT's words that 'the TUPE Regulations continue to yield fresh problems particularly in the area of the contracting out of services by public authorities' might never have been so apt, at least in the *Tuck* case if not in the future.

The wider definition of business transfer adopted by *Rask* shows that TUPE does apply to contracting-out. Successive restatements of this position clearly enunciated in *Schmidt*, *Dines* and *Wren* have major implications for the UK government's contracting-out policy. In essence, employees affected by contracting-out now retain their continuity of employment. Local and health authorities et al., the previous providers, are now liable for redundancy payments; new contractors will be expected to continue contractually agreed salaries and terms; and, most significantly, any dismissal connected with contracting-out transfers will be deemed automatically unfair, unless the ETO defences apply. As a result, private contractors will no longer be able to submit successful tender bids on the basis of lower labour costs, since the ARD ensures that terms and conditions of employment are unchanged, except, of course, pension provisions which remain untransferable. Thus contracting-out's rationale centred on reducing public expenditure could be fatally undermined. Contractors will now simply be unwilling to make bids without an indemnity for dismissal costs and redundancies from the previous provider.

An analogy arises between the ETO defences within the legal framework for business transfers with that of unfair dismissal law's 'some other substantial reason' (SOSR). The admissible SOSR justification was introduced into the unfair dismissal law framework in the 1970s, due to the sufferance of an economic downturn in that period. The analogy between 'SOSR' and TUPE's ETO defences becomes clearer when placed in the context of the 'economic reality' of the circumstances and the employer's decision. There are, in fact, 92 cases to date which concern the usage of the SOSR defence. Recent decisions, such as *Dines*, highlighted that employers are more likely now to offer ETO defences more readily. Since the *Dines* decision, albeit a victory for the unions, an indirect message to business that the ETO defences would have a greater role in the future of transfers has become widespread. Thus, both the *Dines* and *Tuck* decisions might offer a disguised rekindling of the SOSR for transferors and transferees alike, so as to help them evade any liabilities which might arise under TUPE. As a consequence, in the 1990s the ETO defences might be as successful as SOSR throughout the 1970s–80s in the UK.

As this text has already identified, differing judicial attitudes emerge amid the respective approaches adopted by the UK and EU judges. The EU judges have adopted a 'purposive' interpretation which has reluctantly been adopted by the UK judiciary. Previously, the UK judges' approach can be traced back to their support of the widely-used 'managerial prerogative', meaning that the reason of 'business efficacy' is used to justify employers' policies. From a discussion of the case law it emerges that a revival in the importance of economics, alongside an anticipated wider usage of the ETO defences, as implied in the *Dines* and *Tuck* decisions, shows that the British tradition, enshrined in laissez-faire and the freedom of contract, could prevail. However, as UK judges acquaint themselves, like both their EU and US counterparts, with some basic economic thinking following the *Ratcliffe* case, the EU teleological approach might even prevail in UK judicial deliberations. Given that only twelve cases, since 1983 to date, have considered the importance of these ETO defences, then an upturn in this trend is likely following *Dines*. The economic aspect of the ETO defences could therefore have been widened, particularly with regard to contracting-out business transfers, business transfers under contracting-out exercises being undeniably a result of economic circumstances. The main reason why an increase in the usage of these defences is anticipated is the fact that the terms themselves, 'economic', 'technical' or 'organisational', are not defined. Like the SOSR justification, the ETO defences remain sufficiently vague as to allow the users of these defences to mould them as their discretion sees fit. It also allows the courts and tribunals a discretion to decide what is reasonable when utilised. The EAT's latest guidance on the usage of the SOSR justification requires a focus upon the extent to which the dismissals or redundancies are due to the reason given.

This guidance does very little to prevent the usage of the ETO defences when confronted with a contracting-out business transfer. The EAT instituting its new test for SOSR found that even where a sound 'business reason' is given, a balancing process between the disadvantages of the new terms to the employees and the advantages to the employers must be undertaken. In light of the last test, one might argue that the ETO defences might even be restricted in a contracting-out context, restricted in so far as, even where the employer can justify the less favourable terms as a consequence of the mechanics of contracting-out, where the disadvantages to the employee are worsened to the employer's advantage, an ETO defence might even then be rejected as unreasonable.

As already mentioned, the fact that the primary legislation is committed to safeguarding employees' rights, but simultaneously provides employers with defences, means that these ETO, when reasonably deployed, can defeat the legislation's aim. This somewhat inconsistent approach is the consequence of an EU compromise to assist employees while remaining 'fair' to employers. However, what remains a salient fact is that these defences could potentially present the next wave of litigation on the law relating to business transfers.

Summary

In the context of either contracting-out or contracting-in, the law seeks to protect workers, while underlying market forces seek to simultaneously challenge workers' rights and job security. With 'Best Value' as CCT's successor since January 2000, outsourcing will continue in various forms and now local authorities and others have to demonstrate that they have the most effective method of providing services (i.e. have achieved 'best value'). But what is 'best value' and will the ETO defences present further flexibility for employers, especially providers, in any event? In any case, the fact that little attention has been drawn to the ETO defences demonstrates in a British context how UK lawyers and HR practitioners alike need to utilise their interpretation skills at work.

To sum up, contracting-out involves facilities management, contract services, or compulsory competitive tendering and best value. Today, the implications of 'best value' are, in business transfer terms, that new terms mean the repudiation of the contract, that consent to new terms may not necessarily be binding, and that the duration of TUPE protection does dilute with time.

However, the central message of the courts has been that deliberate avoidance is unworkable. In any event, anti-avoidance provisions exist within TUPE, so that no contracting out of or waiver of TUPE should occur. The ETO defences provide the flexibility required to facilitate change and are defined as:

- economic – market driven/business needs;

- technical – technological advancement;

- organisational – structures, no need for duplication.

In the next chapter, the collective issues surrounding consultation and information will be considered.

CHAPTER 5

Information and consultation issues

The ECJ's 1994 ruling in *Commission* v. *UK* requiring the UK to implement its obligations under the ARD and Collective Redundancies Directive 75/129 into national law raised important questions about information, consultation and representation in relation to business transfers. In response to this ruling, the UK government announced its proposals on workers' representatives. This revision arises from Terry Wren's action against Eastbourne Borough Council. Wren and other refuse collectors and street cleaners were given redundancy payments following a contracting-out exercise in the cleaning section of the borough council under the Local Government Act 1988. The EAT upheld Wren and others' appeal and remitted it to another ET for reconsideration. The major issue of concern to Wren and others was their lack of information and Eastbourne Borough Council's failure to consult them.

The issue of the provision of information and consultation to workers subjected to business transfers could become further confused with the advent of European Works Councils (EWCs) across the EU under Council Directive 94/45/EC. This directive provides a legislative framework for the establishment of EWCs in transnational undertakings, which some 138 major UK companies have opted to voluntarily implement. Consequently, this chapter will address the key provisions on consultation and information relating to business transfers, as well as the rights to representation.

Key TUPE provisions on collective rights

TUPE contains provisions intended to facilitate constructive relations between employers (both transferor and transferee) and trade unions/elected representatives. The effect of Regulations 6, 9 and 10 is to preserve the existing collective bargaining arrangements on sale of the business.

- *Regulation 6* requires that any collective agreement made between the transferor and a trade union shall have effect as if it had been made with the transferee.

- *Regulation 9* provides that any trade union which was recognised by the transferor shall be deemed to be recognised by the transferee.

- *Regulation 10* obliges the transferor and transferee to consult with recognised trade unions or elected representatives (in the absence of a recognised trade union) for the purposes of collective consultation under TUPE.

Following the enactment of the 1999 Employment Relations Act and the institution of legal procedures for the recognition of trade unions within the workplace where there are sufficient members of the workforce who are trade union members, as well as derecognition procedures, then Regulation 9 may become more complex and may have to respond to the pace of change brought about by this new legal framework. However, public sector agreements on trade union recognition are more common than private sector arrangements. Consequently, under TUPE the transferee is normally bound by the existing collective agreements and recognition arrangements, but under the 1999 Act the transferee may be able to terminate or modify the arrangements inherited. For instance, the transferee may seek derecognition.

However, the transferee may have difficulties changing those terms of collective agreements which have already been incorporated into individual employees' contracts, as these, once incorporated, will become binding. As a result any subsequent changes to collective agreements have to be agreed at a collective level. Alternatively, the transferee can alter a collective agreement which is not legally binding unless it contains a clause indicating that it has legal effect.

Consultation and informing

As noted above Regulation 10 of TUPE sets an obligation to collectively consult before a business transfer. Under Regulation10 the transferor must inform and consult with 'appropriate representatives' of affected employees, i.e. those employees subjected to the transfer or by measures taken in connection with the transfer. This means that all those being transferred should be consulted/informed, but also other employees who are not transferring but are affected should be consulted. For example, if the secretarial support team is being transferred, these would all be consulted, as would the clerical staff who support them as the transfer would also affect their job function.

Another issue arising in this connection concerns who are 'appropriate representatives'? Regulation 9 may provide the answer – recognised trade unions. However, where no trade unions are recognised, then elected representatives must be in place (this is to be discussed below in detail). Central to consultation is the requirement that the transferee provide information to the transferor to inform the workforce. Where recognised trade unions are in place the consultation process should be relatively straightforward. However, where no such unions exist, identifying 'appropriate representatives' must be overcome by the transferor. This may not be that easy. For instance, even where trade unions are recognised, the transferor must ensure that the union represents all the employees who are affected. This does not mean that they have to be members of that trade union, but that the union concerned represents them in respect of the transfer.

However, from July 1999, the Collective Redundancies and Transfer of Undertakings (Protection of Employment) (Amendment) Regulations 1999, to be discussed below, set out new requirements for consultation for transfers post 1 November 1999 where no recognised unions exist. Such new Regulations resolve the problem of identifying 'appropriate representatives'.

Challenges to collective rights

The central concern of the *EC Commission* v. *UK* ruling is the obligation in the ARD to consult employees recognised as employee representatives, an obligation of which the UK was found in breach. The UK government must therefore provide some means or mechanism by which non-employee representatives will be consulted. The TUC prefers a Code of Practice, whereas the UK government's response is to establish an ad hoc representatives scheme. This ruling has placed much more emphasis on the issue of representation in terms of consultation being the key to safeguarding rights under business transfers. This ECJ ruling, however, poses mixed blessings, since it addresses the issue of consultation which can be achieved by mixed systems of elected representatives or representative unions. The UK's response was to argue that individual rights are better than collective rights, since who otherwise negotiates for non-union members?

The fundamental problem is the definitional ambiguity which surrounds the term 'representativeness' in a workplace context. What does it mean in the employment environment? The response to that question is determined by answering two further questions: whether trade unions should have participation rights in a workplace dialogue and, where it is accepted that trade unions have these rights, what forms of dialogue, or mechanisms, are in place? This reasoning also encounters a further difficulty in so far as we must define what a 'trade union' is. This is problematical because there are three options to explore before answering the question. The options available can either take the statutory definition found in s. 1 of the TULRCA 1992, or whether 'trade union' status depends upon registration as a union or, alternatively, whether it depends upon certification or legal recognition under the 1999 Act.

However, given English law's current stance, management often determine what is meant by 'representativeness', which is usually dependent upon which union is recognised, if any, for bargaining purposes.

As a concept, 'representativeness' is important for collective bargaining reasons. Information channels are indeed vital to those workers subjected to transfers. Despite these ideals for 'representativeness' and its consultation and bargaining functions, the trend today in the UK is towards derecognition and falling unionisation rates. In contrast, the EU is creating social partnership and promoting social dialogue. In a British context, the TUC has recently reclaimed statutory recognition rights. As representativeness is directly linked to membership levels and currently where trade union density is less than 30% and less than 50% of the workforce are covered by collective bargaining, UK employers are either more willing, or have no other choice but, to hold workplace elections. This is, however, not unique to the UK. In France, plant level elections take place as a means of determining what and who is 'representative' for bargaining purposes. These problems might explain the reasons behind the UK's reluctance to accept the ECJ's ruling and the consultation obligations provided for in the ARD and TUPE. The UNISON case R. v. Secretary of State for Transport, ex parte UNISON (1996), involving the business transfer of a hospital to NHS trust status, showed that even if an employer does not fulfil the requisite consultation regulations, then the sanction of four weeks' pay compensation does very little as a deterrent (now 13 weeks' pay).

The 1995 Regulations

The 1995 Regulations controversially came into force on 26 October 1995 and applied to transfers before 1 November 1999. They were introduced in the UK Parliament on 5 October 1995, then debated at 10 o'clock in the evening in the House of Lords as a Prayer of Annulment. It took the UK government 16 months to produce them and yet these new Regulations did not fully comply with the ECJ's ruling in 1994. Three specific deregulatory measures were unnecessarily put into these Regulations, including an obligation to consult only where there are 20 or more employees; consultation will take place at the 'earliest opportunity' and where 'reasonably practicable to do so', rather than as the 1975 Collective Redundancies Directive prescribes 'in good time'; and the EAT's judgment in the *Milligan* v. *Securicor* (1995) case was reversed (the EAT held that where a dismissal by transfer occurred, it was not subject to the two-year qualifying period).

The Regulations themselves required employers to consult their employees about collective redundancies and business transfers. Regulation 3(2) provided for consultation between employer and employees, though Regulations 6 and 11 allow for a choice between recognised unions or an elected staff body, giving employers a much wider discretion than before. These Regulations therefore did not comply with the ECJ's ruling because they allow an opportunity for employers to not fully consult with their employees. The overall aim of the ECJ's ruling was to curb such non-consultation practices, such practices being legitimately and legally allowed to unfold because of the choice given to employers to determine whether to select a trade union for the purposes of consultation or to elect representatives. UK employers no longer have to derecognise unions, safe in the knowledge that unions can be ignored. Again the question as to which of these is more representative arises, and again this depends upon the workplace concerned. These Regulations therefore instituted an ad hoc arrangement, as advanced by the Advocate-General in the *EC Commission* v. *UK* case. The 1995 Regulations '…represented a grudging, minimalist response to the ECJ's decision, coupled with anti-union and deregulatory measures to sugar the pill'.

The problems did not end there. After employers have decided whether to consult elected bodies or existing trade unions, what type of agreement is to be reached? The 1977 Directive required such consultation with a view to 'seeking agreement'. The crucial point here is one concerning independence. Clearly any definition of 'independence' is one involving employees not being under the control of the employer, although, in terms of elected representatives, no independence is statutorily required, unlike that required of trade unions. The ECJ's judgment on this point specifically outlawed the 'free choice of employers', whereas the 1995 Regulations installed a choice for employers, and this produces a crucial defect. Moreover, the Regulations created a 'new' regulation, Regulation 3(8), which fixed a time limit which the Directive did not legislate. New Regulation 3(8) inserted the words 'reasonably practicable', which could mean 10, 90 or 100 days, as no specific limit is enacted. Contrary to other collective legislation in the UK, the 1995 Regulations did not impose any requirement for secret or postal ballots for representative elections. The 1995 Regulations could be seen to have undermined the previous conditions for consultation in the event of business transfers. They clearly do not comply with the ECJ's ruling, nor do they produce an effective scheme of consultation. The lack of independence of employee representatives and no description of any electoral scheme or process required produces no genuine conditions for reaching agreement.

Consequently, those affected by the 1995 Regulations sought to challenge them. The less than 20 employees threshold has proved to be the most controversial of these measures. The fragmented nature of the British labour force made it easier to find workplaces where there are 20 employees or less. As a result, the NASUWT, along with the GMB and UNISON, challenged the 1995 Regulations by way of judicial review. These joined judicial review actions challenged the legality of the new Regulations when read together with ss. 188–98 of TULRCA 1992 and the TUPE Regulations 1981.

The NASUWT's concerns arose primarily out of the tight and restricted timescale for consultation about these Regulations which are now in force. Their major concern was that they were (in fact are) a recognised union for teachers working for a variety of employers in grant-maintained, voluntary-aided and LEA schools and colleges. In the context of education, some schools, particularly in the voluntary-aided sector, might have less than 20 employees. In these schools no consultation for redundancies or transfers would have been required, although redundancies can occur under s. 188 of TULRCA 1992. The EAT ruled in the *National Union of Teachers* v. *Governing Body of St Mary's Church of England (Aided) Junior School* (1997) case that a school does not amount to 'an undertaking' for the purposes of TUPE protection, unless the body against which the school is bringing the action is deemed 'an emanation of state'. In the instant case, the Aided Junior School was found not to be 'an emanation of state'. However, the Court of Appeal later included such schools as emanations of state on the basis that the formula established in *Foster* v. *British Gas Plc* (1991) was much wider and more exclusive than the criteria which were erroneously applied by the EAT. This is an issue which was of great concern in the business transfers debate until 1992 when NATFHE took action and the courts resolved that union recognition is transferable in the event of business transfers under the ARD.

In the High Court, three unions, UNISON, GMB and the NASUWT, sought a declaration that the 1995 Regulations were incompatible with the Directives on Collective Redundancies and Business Transfers and thus unlawful. In particular, the applicant unions sought to deem that Regulations 3(2) and 8 were *ultra vires* the powers of the Secretary of State. The applicants argued that the exclusion from the scope of the Regulations of redundancies affecting a single employee was contrary to existing law contained in both Article 1(1) of the Collective Redundancies Directive and s. 188(1), TULRCA 1992 which protects individuals. In addition, these Regulations also had a disparate adverse impact on women contrary to the Equal Treatment Directive 76/207. As a consequence, the Regulations complained of were contrary to the UK's obligations conferred under Articles 5 and 117 of the Treaty of Rome. In response, the UK government submitted that they had acted *intra vires* having amended the TUPE Regulations and TULRCA 1992 in light of the *EC Commission* v. *UK* case, and that moreover, the new ss. 188(1) and (2) providing for consultation where an employer proposes to make 20 or more employees redundant over a period of

90 days or less and the two-year continuous qualification period were lawful. Lastly, the UK government rejected any prima facie case of indirect discrimination against women.

The High Court's decision, per Otton LJ and Newman J, not to grant the order of certiorari was based on the grounds that the Regulations fully complied with the UK's obligations under s. 2(2), ECA 1972. On the specific issue of consultation and election, the Court held that '...the employer is deemed to comply if he has invited employees to elect representatives and given enough time to allow for elections', and thus the 1995 Regulations were found to be lawful. Unions could therefore be legally sidestepped by elected representatives when it comes to consultation about business transfers. As the court concluded: 'I am not persuaded that the Regulations are defective in that they did not provide more detail for the election of representatives'. Though Otton LJ did not set out a subjective test for the selection of 'appropriate representatives', the High Court maintained that objectivity still remained and that an individual employee could claim that inadequate consultation took place as an inappropriate employee was chosen as a representative. This effectively meant that an employer cannot easily discharge the burden for consultation unless employees neglect to take up the offer to elect representatives. It was expected that employers would be encouraged to establish formal consultation machinery, even recognise unions, following this decision, in order to convince tribunals and courts alike that they meet the requirements set out by the law. The court also upheld the two-year qualification period as '...*employees with less than two years were a "specific category"* of employee within the meaning of the [ARD]' and that the applicants had not made out a prima facie case of discrimination with regard to the restriction of consultation to redundancies of more than 20 employees.

Similarly in *R. v. Secretary of State for the Environment, ex parte Oswestry Borough Council* (1994), the High Court dismissed the Council's application for judicial review. In this case, the Secretary of State directed the Council to include in their tender invitations for contracts for their refuse collection a clause that the successful tenderer must employ the Council's existing workforce on their existing terms and conditions. Challenging this direction, the Council argued that these instructions were unreasonable. The High Court deemed the Secretary of State's direction reasonable and not illegal. Accordingly, the High Court dismissed the applications. Even so, the EU Commission remained concerned that these Regulations did not satisfy the requirements of EC law, as decreed by the ECJ. Consequently, infraction proceedings were commenced by the EU Commission and in 1998 the UK government decided to repeal and amend the 1995 Regulations.

The 1999 Regulations

The 1999 Regulations came into force from 1 November 1999. These Regulations ended much of the uncertainty presented in the provisions of the 1995 Regulations and require that information be given to and consultation take place with trade union representatives if the employees affected are represented by a recognised trade union. Where no such trade union exists or applies, the transferor can choose whether to inform/consult with employee representatives who have been elected and hold the authority to receive information and be consulted on behalf of affected employees, or to hold elections for ad hoc representatives for the purposes of the TUPE transfers. As a result these Regulations establish two key stages for information and consultation:

- *Stage 1.* Prior to the consultation, where no recognised trade union applies, the transferor and transferee should take the following steps:

    – Consider the number of representatives required.

    – Correspond with all employees affected (including those absent or on sick leave) and request nominations.

    – Correspond with nominees and confirm 'willingness'.

    – Explain the role of elected representatives to nominees.

    – Distribute secret ballot forms to all employees affected.

    – Count the ballot and notify representatives.

- *Stage 2.* Having elected the representatives, the transferor/ transferee should take the following steps:

    – Meet with the representatives.

    – Ensure that the elected representatives meet with other employees to establish views.

    – Consider representatives' views.

    – Confirm outcomes to all employees.

Note that where an employer does all the above steps but fails to attain elected representatives for whatever reasons although a genuine opportunity to elect such representatives has occurred, then the employer has discharged his duty/obligations under TUPE. Proof of such, though, will be required should this be challenged in the future. Therefore keeping records of meetings etc. is essential. The key here is to establish a reasonable time schedule.

Regulation 10(3) requires the transferee to notify the transferor of any measures envisaged taking affect after the transfer so as to enable this information to be given to the affected employees, though the transferee is not obliged to consult prior to the transfer with those affected by the transfer.

It is important that, under the 1999 Regulations, at all times the transferor should consider the following practical implications to ensure 'proper' informing and consulting is taking place:

- whether the agreed arrangements for information/ consultation cover all the employees affected;

- whether sufficient time has been given at all stages (nominations, elections, meetings);

- whether the employees can 'freely vote' (i.e. no intimidation etc.);

- confirm total number of employees who must be represented and the various locations and subdivisions;

- clarify the terms of office of the representatives;

- confirm 'confidentiality' rules regarding consultation/information with the elected representatives;

- utilise an independent scrutineer to count ballot(s).

One problem may remain for certain types of transfer, that is those that are commercially sensitive. To seek to elect ad hoc representatives for a 'sensitive transfer' may be difficult. Consequently, two options are available: (a) convert an existing body into a body of representatives for consultation (e.g. another permanent body, such as an EWC or a Health and Safety Committee); or (b) consult with individual employees on a direct basis. (See the *Humphreys* v. *University of Oxford* (2000) case for an example.) This situation of secrecy will be particularly true where the Stock Exchange Rules on Mergers and Take-Overs applies. In such circumstances non-compliance with TUPE may be justified where a breach of other regulatory rules would occur (see Regulation 10(7) – Special Circumstances Defence). These exceptions, however, are likely to be narrowily construed by the courts/tribunals.

Above all the 1999 Regulations require the transferor to ensure that 'the elections are fair and that sufficient representatives to represent the interests of all affected employees are in place and that the requisite information and consultation is completed'.

Practical issues post-1999 Regulations

A number of practical issues arise in consequence of the 1999 Regulations, such as the rights of the elected representatives, timescales, information obligations, consultation rights and remedies.

Elected representatives

Once elected the employer must provide facilities and assistance. For example, good access must be given to the relevant employees/workforce(s). Elected representatives also have the right to paid time-off during the working day to execute their duties as a representative or undergo training. Note also that any dismissals of elected representatives will be treated as automatically unfair if the reason is that the employee was an elected representative under TUPE (or standing as a nominee in a ballot for elected representatives under TUPE). No such elected representatives should suffer any detriment while undertaking their duties or function as an elected representative.

Timescales

It is imperative that throughout the consultation process reasonable time is given. Regulation 10(2) provides that information about the transfer *must* be given to the representatives 'long before the transfer to enable consultation to take place'. While TUPE does not set out clear timescales, transferors should be careful not to rush the process. Unlike redundancy consultation where timescales are set, clearly TUPE implicitly requires 'meaningful dialogue' about the economic, social and legal implications. 'Good time' may mean 30 days or more (following the redundancy model) to allow for consultation 'with a view to reaching agreement' on the key issues.

Information obligations

Regulation 10(2) provides that the transferor should provide the elected representatives with information on: the facts of the transfer (date and reasons); the 'legal, social and economic' implications (as perceived by the transferee) for the affected employees; what measures are envisaged, post-transfer; and any other information provided or measures envisaged by the transferee. Regulation 10(3) requires the transferee to notify the transferor of any information appropriate to be given to the elected representatives. What often troubles those involved in transfers here is not the openness, but the technical terms 'measures' and 'envisaged'. In the case of *IPCS* v. *Secretary of State for Defence* (1987), it was held that the term 'measures' encompassed any action or step envisaged by the employer as affecting the transferred employees, for example consequential redundancies or alterations to working practices or contracts of employment. Moreover, 'envisaged' was considered to mean a measure formulated from a proposal or coherent plan relating to the business transfer.

Consultation rights

Regulation 10(5) requires that consultation should be conducted 'with a view to seeking the [elected] representatives' agreement to measures to be taken'. To that end, consultation only commences following information which leads to the transferor/transferee envisaging taking measures in connection with the transfer (i.e. redundancies, changes to contracts, changes to working conditions/practices, union derecognition or union recognition, or any changes whatsoever). Once consultation commences TUPE implies that all proposed measures should be discussed in good faith and that every effort be made to accommodate views and differences and reach agreement where possible. Such a requirement establishes a collective bargaining model.

Remedies

Any breach of Regulation 10 gives a right of complaint to an ET under Regulation 11 on the grounds of failure to comply (i.e. electoral defects; no or lack of information; no, limited or lack of consultation; lack of trade union recognition; or any other case affecting employees). Where an ET upholds the complaint, a declaration is given and the transferor will be required to pay 13 weeks' pay (prior to 1/11/99 it was four weeks under the 1995 Regulations, as noted above) to each employee affected. Note that the week's pay is *not* subject to the maximum limit of £260 per week for these purposes. Note that s. 7 of the 1998 Local Government Act requires open competition. For those service providers in the public sector, non-compliance with consultation could potentially be deemed anti-competitive behaviour.

Francovich claims

The Francovich Doctrine, following from the *Francovich* v. *Italian Republic* (1992) case, provides an extra legal means by which an EU member state can be sued for its failure to fully implement a directive. In order to bring such a claim the aggrieved EU national must demonstrate detrimental loss and that the loss is attributable to the failure of the EU member state's government to implement the directive comprehensively. Such state liability has been elaborated upon in the *Brasserie du Pêcheur* (1996) case, where it added that where the EU member state disregarded its discretion to enact the legislation as it sees best to fulfil its EU legislative obligations, then serious breach has occurred.

Consequently, for a successful Francovich action, four conditions must be met:

1.   Applicant must show that the relevant directive grants rights to individuals.

2.   Those rights are identifiable on the basis of the directive's provisions.

3.   There is a causal link between the breach of the EU member state's obligations and the detriment incurred.

4.   The EU member state concerned did 'gravely and manifestly' disregard the limits on its discretion to implement the directive.

Applying such a doctrine to the ARD provides litigants with another right of claim. In fact, some 188 writs were lodged against the UK for breach of consultation rights. Clearly EU governments, and particularly the UK government, need to ensure that they give full effect to directives, including the ARD (this will become important in Chapter 7). In a collective context, UK trade unions could make full usage of these damages where the ARD is implemented improperly. Moreover, UK employers might explore the application of *Francovich* as a defence for their non-compliance where they believe that they have adhered to the UK provisions.

Summary

As observed in the recent sale of Rover by BMW, the collective issues surrounding business transfers are becoming increasingly important, as the future role for workplace consultation becomes more relevant alongside the greater likelihood that Works Councils and union recognition will grow in numbers throughout the UK. Following the final decision given by Brighton ET in the *Wren* (1993) case, resulting in the awarding of £131,000 compensation for Tony Wren and another 16 former dustmen after six years of litigation involving two ET and two EAT hearings, the collective rights contained in TUPE have been maintained and therefore no employer can afford to ignore the sanction of 13 weeks' compensation per employee. In any event, good consultation and information is the key to a successful transfer.

To sum up, the key collective provisions are:

- Regulation 6 – collective agreements;

- Regulation 9 – trade union recognition;

- Regulation 10 – information/consultation;

- Regulation 11 – remedies.

Collective agreements, in order to apply, must be incorporated into the contract and consequently they are binding on the new employer.

TU recognition is covered in Regulation 9, as now supplemented by the Employment Relations Act 1999 which revitalises collective bargaining. However, the 1999 Consultation Regulations, effective since 1 November 1999, ensure that employers consult with either trade unions or elected representatives to ensure that those affected by the transfer are consulted. By way of deterrence, a sanction of some 13 weeks' pay applies where there is non-compliance. In terms of the information to be given to TUs or elected representatives, it must be 'in good time', cover the legal, economic and social implications and set out the measures envisaged. Consultation must therefore take place 'with a view to reaching agreement', occur within a reasonable timescale, and include a discussion on the changes/'measures envisaged' (e.g. redundancies).

CHAPTER 6

Recent legal developments and some business solutions

Anyone involved in TUPE will know that the pace of change is immense. Since we are dealing with a 'moving target' as subject-matter this chapter provides some recent legal developments. Furthermore, this chapter seeks to present some business solutions that form good practice when dealing with some of the TUPE issues discussed so far.

Recent case law developments

The following sections relate back to Chapters 2–5 and highlight the recent legal developments.

Life after **Suzen** *(1997) and some more ECJ rulings*

The joined cases of *Francisco Hernandez* v. *Gomez* and *Sanchez Hildago* v. *Asociación De Servicios and Sociedad Cooperativa Minerva* were the first ECJ rulings post *Suzen* in 1999. In these cases the ECJ began to soften the *Suzen* decision. The focus in these rulings was on whether an economic entity was transferred, as opposed to whether a major part of the workforce had been transferred as in *Suzen*. Consequently, this new approach by the court lay emphasis on what the undertaking looked like pre-transfer rather than post-transfer. The ECJ held that 'an organized grouping of wage earners who were specifically and permanently assigned a common task may amount to an economic entity' and consequently the ARD (a.k.a. TUPE) applies in such circumstances. More recently, the ECJ in *Collino and Chiappero* (2000) ruled that the ARD applies to all entities that carry on economic activities, irrespective of whether they operated for profit prior to transfer or not. This case involved the Italian state-owned telecom service being awarded to a private company in 1992 and then, after a reorganization, becoming Telecom Italia. The dispute surrounded the transfer of continuous service. On this point the ECJ confirmed that account should be taken of entire length of service. Similarly, in *Mayeur* v. *Association Promotion de L'Information Messine* (2000), concerning a non-profit tourist information service whose function was transferred to the local authority in 1997, Mayeur was dismissed and claimed unfair dismissal. The result was that the ECJ reaffirmed that the ARD applies to the transfer of an economic activity from private to public or public to private. In *Mayeur* it ruled that an economic function was transferred rather than an administrative activity. In this case the ARD applied so long as the service retained its identity post-transfer.

More confusion was created on 25 January 2001, when the ECJ in *Oy Liikenne Ab* v. *Liskojarvi and Juntunen* (2001), a transfer involving the contracting-out of Finnish buses, concluded that because no buses had been transferred no transfer could have occurred. Despite transferring 33 of the 45 employees, none of the 26 buses nor other assets were transferred and the ECJ as a result ruled that while labour-intensive operations might be subjected to a transfer, other factors had to be considered where the undertaking depended on the use of substantial assets. To that end, the ECJ took the view that a bus service operation needed buses and therefore the provision of a such a service could not be viewed as a service based on labour alone. In this case, a contracting-out transfer was excluded from the Directive/TUPE's remit. Clearly, reform of the ARD since 1998 has had little affect on the ECJ's jurisprudential approach.

What constitutes a transfer?

In the case of *Cheeseman* v. *Brewer* (2000) the EAT held that the ET had failed to take account of the existing case law. More significantly, it failed to look at things 'in the round'. In particular it had failed to consider whether the undertaking had retained its identity.

This case highlights how ETs must take account of the ECJ's rulings and that they should apply common sense to proceedings while applying the relevant legal tests (as discussed in Chapter 2).

Determining that TUPE applies!

The Court of Session in *Lightways (Contractors) Ltd* v. *Associated Holdings Ltd* (2000) held that where the parties to the business transfer had made it clear that TUPE would apply, then TUPE did apply. Inversely, in situations where the parties agreed that TUPE would not apply, this would not be so (see *ECM* v. *Cox* (1998), no avoidance of TUPE ruling).

Consultation, dismissals and TUPE

The Court of Appeal, as noted in Chapters 2 and 4, held in *ECM* v. *Cox* (1998) that the *Suzen* case had been overstated. Such was the conclusion in *Kerry Foods* v. *Creber* (2000), where a sausage-maker was closed down by receivers and all the existing staff were made redundant, yet the business was sold and Kerry Foods began production using the previous brand name but none of the former staff were employed. It was held that a relevant transfer had occurred and that the dismissals were connected to the transfer. Consequently, the transferor had to pay compensation to the employees, including an award for failure to consult.

Contracting-out after Suzen

In both the *ADI (UK) Ltd* v. *Willer* and *Whitewater Leisure Management Ltd* v. *Barnes* (2000) cases where the contracting-out of services had occurred, in applying the *Suzen* ruling the UK EAT held that as no material assets transferred and a majority of the workforce did not transfer there could not be a business transfer.

Clearly such cases clarify the headache left by *Suzen* in that following these decisions labour-intensive transfers are not covered by TUPE. Consequently, the fact that no material assets can be shown to have been transferred results in no transfer of undertaking and therefore TUPE cannot apply.

Subsidiaries and transfers

In *Allen* v. *Amalgamated Construction Co Ltd* (2000) the ECJ ruled that the ARD applied to a transfer between two subsidiary companies within the same group where there were distinct legal personalities, i.e. each had specific employment relationships with their respective employees.

ECM and afterwards

In *ECM (Vehicle Delivery Services) Ltd* v. *Cox* (1999) multiple transfers took place and the final transferee refused to take on the original transferred staff in order to avoid the application of TUPE. The ET held that TUPE still applied and this was confirmed by the Court of Appeal. Since *ECM*, the EAT held in the case of *OCS Cleaning (Scotland) Ltd* v. *Rudden and Olscot Ltd* (1999) that TUPE applied even where there was no transfer of assets or none of the existing staff taken on, the reason for applying TUPE being the presence of work which was substantially the same as before the transfer (i.e. for the same customer at the same place). While these factors are not conclusive themselves, the message sent out from this decision was that contractors must be aware of a real risk that, on any outsourcing or changeover of contractors, TUPE would apply. This approach was confirmed in *RCO Support Services* v. *UNISON* (2000), where the EAT held that ancillary services are often staffed by workers with only relatively simple and commonly available skills on which account TUPE could apply. Note that *ECM* v. *Cox* was followed in *Magna Housing Association* v. *Turner* (1998). However, since the Court of Appeal's ruling in the *ECM* v. *Cox* case, the EAT has held in *OCS Cleaning (Scotland) Ltd* v. *Rudden and Olscot Ltd* (1999) that TUPE may apply in cases where there has not been a transfer of assets or where no existing staff are taken on by the new employer.

Defining the 'economic' in ETO

In *Wheeler* v. *Patel* (1987) it was determined that for an economic reason to fall within the ETO defences (Regulation 8(2)) it must relate to the conduct of the business and not the sale of the business. However, in *Whitehouse* v. *Blatchford* (1999) the EAT held that where the grant of a contract to the transferee was made conditional upon a reduction in the workforce then a dismissal in order to obtain a contract was distinct from a dismissal to secure a business transfer. The transfer was therefore merely the event for the dismissal and not the cause. Hence ETO applied. A dismissal can be for 'ETO' reasons even if the dismissal would not have been made but for the business transfer, as was the case in *Trafford* v. *Sharpe* (1994) and *Warner* v. *Adnet Ltd* (1998). Yet in *Kerry Foods* v. *Creber* (2000), the EAT decided that if the business transfer is the effective reason for the dismissal then the ETO defences should not apply, although, if the transfer was a reason for the dismissal, then the dismissal itself would not be automatically unfair. It is suggested that readers should be wary of the *Kerry Foods* decision given that it is potentially inconsistent with TUPE and therefore incorrect.

Out and in – which contract is transferred?

In *MoD* v. *Clutterbuck* (2000) the EAT held that the last contract worked under is the contract transferred. For example, in this case, Clutterbuck was originally employed by the MoD before being transferred, i.e. contracted out, to a private contractor and was later transferred back, i.e. contracted-in, to the MoD. The case centred on which direction the contract had been transferred: the MoD contract to the private contractor or vice versa. It was decided that the private contractor contract had been transferred to the MoD.

Collective agreements post-transfer

What happens to collective agreements after transfer was the question posed in *Williams West* v. *Fairgrieve* (2000). The EAT replied that the contracts should be read as referring to collective agreements between the transferee and the trade union/individual. Therefore, agreements reached between the transferor and the trade union do *not* become incorporated into contracts between the employees and the new employer (the transferee), contrary to custom and practice.

Dismissals and TUPE

A dismissal is automatically unfair only if it is connected to the business transfer (Regulation 8(1)). Note that liability for such dismissals passes from the transferor to the transferee. It was considered that time was the crucial factor, but that this is not so may be observed in *Taylor* v. *Connex South Eastern Ltd* (2000), where the EAT held that even though four years had elapsed since the transfer, the reason for the dismissal two years after the transfer related to the business transfer. This case reminds us that the key term is 'connected to' rather than time.

Constructive dismissal claims and TUPE

In a set of peculiar facts in *Euro-Die UK Ltd* v. *Skidmore* (2000), Skidmore's employment ceased with a company who transferred him to Euro-Die. Before being transferred, Skidmore sought a reassurance that his continuity of employment would be preserved. No reassurance was given. Therefore Skidmore found work elsewhere and claimed constructive dismissal. The EAT upheld the constructive dismissal claim against Euro-Die, the transferee, on the basis on the failure to give a reassurance which amounted to breach of an implied term of trust and confidence. The moral of this story – give reassurances.

Do share options, profit shares and bonus schemes transfer?

It has never been entirely clear whether benefits such as share options, profit shares or bonus schemes transfer. It has often been argued that they do not, since they can be separated from the contract of employment. The EAT in *Unicorn Consultancy Services Ltd* v. *Westbrook* (2000) considered this thorny question and held that these schemes did transfer as contractual rights, though, since the persons in this case were due payments from such schemes during the transfer, the EAT argued that it was entirely within the spirit of TUPE to transfer and make such payments.

Secrecy and consultation

The Court of Appeal in *Humphreys* v. *University of Oxford* (2000) considered a situation where, prior to a transfer, an employee is made aware of the fact that there will be substantial and/or detrimental changes to the contract of employment or working conditions. The court held that the employee could object to the transfer and resign (claiming constructive dismissal against the transferee). The practical point highlighted here is the need for warranties and indemnities (as noted in Chapter 3), as well as the need to consider the transferee informing the staff of his intentions pre-transfer (as questioned in Chapter 5).

Tort liability on transfer

Liability to an employee for personal injury at work arising out of an accident at work prior to a business transfer will transfer to the transferee. The transferee will acquire the benefit of the transferor's employer's liability insurance (albeit that the transferee is *not* party to that insurance). This was the decision of the Court of Appeal in

Bernadone v. *Pall Mall Services Group* (2000), relying upon Regulation 5(2)(a), 'a transferor's right in connection with the contract of employment'.

The case law goes on and on... Save to remind readers to keep abreast of legal developments as they progress.

Some business solutions

So far this guide has presented the legal principles, key issues and practical implications to be mindful of when involved with business transfers. However, to summarise the law and put these legal principles into practice, the following chapter develops a series of suggested processes (a discussion of TUPE strategies will be provided in the concluding Chapter 8) in order to provide some potential/suggested business solutions as guidance alongside good practice which is legally compliant. To help achieve this, the checklists below trace business transfers stage by stage. (Clearly it will also be useful to consult Chapters 1 to 5 for more complete detail where necessary.)

Stage 1 – Pre-transfer

1. Consider if TUPE applies.

2. Examine the liabilities.

3. Consider what transfers.

4. Consider what does *not* transfer.

5. Check the latest legal developments – i.e. the statutory regulations, case law, guidance, etc.

6. Do *not* deliberately avoid TUPE (cf. *ECM* v. *Cox*).

Stage 2 – Contract of sale

1. Undertake a 'due diligence' exercise.

2. Negotiate any relevant indemnities and warranties.

3. Consider the 'pensions' issue (no transfer or comparable provision?).

4. Remember bonuses etc. will be transferred.

5. Check your employer's liability insurance.

Stage 3 – Information/consultation

1. Contact recognised trade union(s) and/or elect representatives for consultation/information purposes.

2. Hold fair and independent elections where necessary by law (i.e. where there is no recognised TU).

3. Provide date and reasons for the transfer.

4. Take 'reasonable time' to inform/consult.

5. Note that the aim of consultation is to 'seek agreement'.

6.   Set out all the legal, economic and social implications.

7.   Negotiate any changes, redundancies and/or dismissals.

8.   Ensure that the transferee sets out 'what is envisaged'.

9.   Note the sanction of 13 weeks' pay per employee (no maximum limit per employee) for non-compliance. (*Always consult!*)

Stage 4 – Dismissals/changing terms

1.   Ascertain the need for dismissals.

2.   Are they connected with the transfer (time lapse is not sufficient alone)?

3.   Dismissals are automatically unfair unless justified (one year qualification).

4.   Remember that the law does not uphold changes to terms post-transfer even if agreed (cf. *Wilson* case).

5.   Harmonisation will be problematical, unless agreed collectively and/or justified, and must not be substantially detrimental.

Stage 5 – Defences (ETO)?

1.   The statutory defences in Regulation 8 are economic, technical or organisational (not related to the sale itself).

2. The defences are related to the conduct of the business.

3. Government guidance states that *economic* relates to a fall in employer's output/can no longer sustain profitability unless dismissals take place; *technical* relates to where the employer wishes to use new technology and employees do not have the necessary skills; *organisational* relates to where the new employer operates at a different location from the previous employer and it is not practical to relocate staff.

4. Any aggrieved employees have a cause of action against the transferee (unfair dismissal – £51,600 maximum limit).

Stage 6 – Post-transfer

1. Check transferees – number of employees required and liabilities.

2. Preserve contracts, trade union recognition and collective agreements.

3. Impose warranties and indemnities if necessary.

4. Plan future business progress.

Stage 7 – Second generation and beyond transfers

1. Return to Stage 1 (note contract transfer as at time of transfer, particularly important re contracting-in).

2.   Take nothing for granted second, third, … time around.

While it is hoped that these checklists will help to summarise matters and provide some succinct guidance, Chapter 8 provides more detailed guidance on TUPE strategies.

Summary

To summarise recent case law:

- *Collino and Chiappero* (2000):

    – economic activity transfer;

    – ARD applies to public to private or private to public;

    – *Suzen* softened – beyond labour intensive transfers;

    – not necessary to have material assets for transfer.

- *Hernandez* and *Hildago* (1999):

    – organised grouping of wage earners;

    – common tasks;

    – applies *Suzen,* but suggest 'major workforce transfer' not sole factor for transfer.

- *ECM* v. *Cox* (1999):

    – Court of Appeal guidance;

    – examine motive where TUPE avoided;

- sanction in avoidance cases = apply TUPE;

- view on TUPE – applicable or not?

- apply TUPE 'carte blanche'?

- non-avoidance is the clear message.

- Post-*ECM* cases:

  - *OCS Cleaning* – contract covered by TUPE (airport cleaning – employers thought TUPE did *not* apply);

  - *RCO Support Services* – protection for vulnerable employees is the aim of TUPE.

- *Humphreys* v. *Oxford University* case:

  - constructive dismissal claim = resignation;

  - can resign when objecting to TUPE transfer;

  - risks for transferor;

  - reassurances?

  - breach of implied term of trust and confidence.

With regard to establishing a link with the transfer, the link between dismissal and transfer may not be related to timing alone (i.e. timing is not decisive). For example, in the *Connex* case there was a 2–4 year gap, but a link was established. Consequently, these developments mean that you must always ensure that the dismissal was not designed to facilitate the sale or reduce costs. Moreover, note that, in order for any such dismissal claims arising from these circumstances to be avoided, the applicant requires one year's continuous employment.

With regard to defences, Article 4 (ARD) and Regulation 8 (TUPE) set out the ETO defences. ECJ guidance has been varied:

- *Abels* (1985): ETO is a valid ground;

- *Bork* (1989): ETO should be used restrictively;

- *D'Urso* (1992): ARD applies if a pre-condition for ETO;

- *Jules Dethier* (1998): 'hands of the transferee are not tied' so can use ETO.

UK decisions have been equally diverse:

- *Berriman* (1985): Court of Appeal noted ETO applies to changes in the workforce;

- *Trafford* v. *Sharpe* (1994): economic reasons outweigh TUPE;

- *BSG Property Services* v. *Tuck* (1996): ETO only applies where ARD applies.

Such mixed messages allow for the need to define/test these defences (risk assessment and strategy).

In establishing business solutions to handling business transfers in the future, legal awareness is the touchstone. More significantly, compliance with the law and applying TUPE are key. In all cases, justify your actions, take 'reasonable time', consider the process and procedures and have reasons. Above all, think long term and avoid litigation.

CHAPTER 7

The future of business transfers

The last three decades have marked the period in which UK employment law and businesses alike faced the consequences of the fragmentation of the British workforce. Given these changes, the law has played an important role in enforcing employers' legal liabilities and employees' rights. This guide has shown that business transfers have been at the forefront of developing modern employment law and practice throughout the EU. In a UK context, business transfers epitomise a legal battle between a pragmatic English legal orthodoxy committed to laissez-faire and a tide of EU regulation. Having discussed the law relating to business transfers, both in their historical and current legal contexts, this chapter now asks what future developments are likely and what dangers face people seeking legal protection under the law governing business transfers. In this chapter the future of business transfers is discussed, given the 1998 Amended Directive and the revised TUPE Regulations 2001, the latter of which have to be in force by the end of July 2001.

The Amended Directive 1998

The 1977 Directive did not prove easy to apply in practice and has proved to be particularly controversial in relation to contracting-out and outsourcing. It has resulted in a significant number of cases being referred from domestic courts to the European Court of Justice for interpretation. The European Commission tendered proposals to amend the original 1977 Directive in 1994. A revised draft was published in 1997 following heavy criticism of the initial proposals by the European Parliament. The most significant change to the original draft was the EU Commission's abandonment of its attempt to clarify the definition of transfer of a business or part of a business by seeking to exclude a transfer of only an activity. Other important proposed amendments related to the liability for pre-transfer debts to employees, the inclusion of state pension provisions within the scope of the ARD while retaining the exclusion of other pensions, the inclusion of insolvency situations and the information and consultation provisions.

A minor success of the UK's Presidency of the Council of Ministers during the first six months of 1998 was to secure the agreement to adopt the Directive amending the Acquired Rights Directive at the Cardiff Summit. The Amended Directive inserts new Articles 1–7b into the 1977 Directive and the revisions must be implemented by EU member states within a three-year period from 29 June 1998 the date of adoption. Let us now consider the amending provisions in detail, analysing the potential implications for employment relations, and identify some missed opportunities in terms of other possible revisions.

Scope of the new Directive

Determining the precise scope of application of the 1977 Directive meant that the European Court of Justice was requested to provide interpretative rulings on a relatively frequent basis. The main problem has been related to the issue of whether the ARD embraces the contracting out of services. In an attempt to clarify matters, the EU Commission had originally proposed adding a new second paragraph to Article 1(1) of the Directive, with the aim of excluding from its scope a transfer of a mere activity of an undertaking as opposed to the transfer an economic entity. The proposal met with substantial criticism from all sides and and it was withdrawn by the EU Commission. Welcoming the deletion the ETUC stated: 'Far from clarifying the law or removing elements of uncertainty, the proposed revision would have made a difficult legal regime almost impossibly complicated and would have diminished workers' rights in the process.'

Unfortunately, the amended formulation which was ultimately adopted, based on words from a number of European cases without relying exclusively on any of them, also offers little in the way of clarification or guidance. Article 1(b) states that there is a transfer 'where there is a transfer of an economic entity which retains its identity, meaning an organised grouping of resources which has the objective of pursuing an economic activity, whether or not that activity is central or ancillary'. Given this inexpansive definition, we are forced to go back to the case law. Indeed, Recital 4 of the Amended Directive specifically emphasizes that the 'clarification' offered by the new Article 1 'does not alter the scope of Directive 77/187/EEC as interpreted by the Court of Justice.' Given that it was the confused state of the case law which prompted demands for a revision to the Directive in the first place, the new definition is of little assistance in meeting its professed aim of clarification in the interests of 'legal security and transparency' (Recital 4).

Recent developments in case law, as seen in Chapter 6, have exacerbated the problem. The ECJ has enunciated the test as to whether a stable economic entity has been transferred. In *Schmidt*, a case involving a first-generation contracting-out, as discussed in Chapter 2, it was held that there could be a transfer of contracted-out cleaning services, even where the services are performed by a single employee and there is no transfer of tangible assets. This approach should be contrasted with the later holding in *Suzen*, a case relating to second-generation contracting-out, that an activity does not, in itself, constitute a stable economic entity. Consequently, the ECJ stated, the mere fact that a similar activity is carried on before and after the change of contractors does not mean that there is a transfer of undertaking. In the case of a labour-intensive undertaking with no significant assets (e.g. contract cleaning) the *Suzen* approach will mean that there will generally be no transfer unless the new contractor takes on the majority of the old contractor's staff. In this decision, the court made no attempt to reconcile its reasoning with the approach adopted in *Schmidt* and signally failed to have regard to the principle of employment protection which underpins the Acquired Rights Directive, opening up a possible evasion strategy for transferee employers. The decision would appear to leave the original 1977 contractor with the choice as to whether to be bound by taking on the majority of the existing staff. Where the existing workforce is unskilled and easily replaceable there is no incentive to assume responsibilities for the existing workforce. The workforce is relegated to the status of mere assets. As a result, the weakest members of the labour market – the unskilled – are disenfranchised from the protection of the acquired rights legislation.

More recently, in the *Hernandez* and *Hidalgo* cases we can observe a possible softening of the *Suzen* approach though with no clarity in this regard. The focus in these rulings is on whether 'an economic entity' has been transferred, as opposed to whether a 'major part of the workforce' has been taken over, as in *Suzen*. This approach seems to lay emphasis on what the undertaking looked like pre-transfer rather than post-transfer and as a result reduces the possibility that a transferee can evade domestic provisions by refusing to engage the employees in the undertaking transferred. In respect of the provision of services, the ECJ holds that 'an organised grouping of wage earners who are specifically and permanently assigned to a common task may, in the absence of other factors of production, amount to an economic entity'.

It is frustrating that these recent rulings do not provide clear guidance. In both decisions, the ECJ adopts word for word the tests approved in *Suzen*. Both *Hernandez* and *Hidalgo* slavishly adopt the *Suzen* test. In order to determine/consider whether the conditions for a transfer of an entity are met, it is necessary to consider all the facts characterising the transaction in question, including in particular the type of undertaking or business, whether or not its tangible assets, such as buildings and movable property, are transferred, the value of its intangible assets at the time of the transfer, *whether or not the majority of its employees are taken over by the new employer*, whether or not its customers are transferred on before and after the transfer, and the period, if any, for which those activities were suspended. However, all those circumstances are merely single factors in the overall assessment which must be made and therefore cannot be considered in isolation.

In a British context, it is suggested that a possible route through this confusion would be to adopt the purposive approach adopted by Mr Justice Morrison in *ECM (Vehicle Delivery Service) Ltd* v. *Cox*, where the court concluded that it would not be proper for a transferee to be able to control the extent of its obligations by refusing to comply with them in the first place. As Mr Justice Morrison stated: 'The issue as to whether employees should have been taken on cannot be determined by asking whether they were taken on.' This approach focuses attention on the motive for refusing to take on the existing workforce, so as to decide whether the motivation was avoidance or for some other reason. Even then, there will be difficult questions of proof in establishing the true motive.

The reasoning in *Suzen* comes very close to the EU Commission's original proposal which sought to distinguish the mere transfer of an activity from the transfer of undertaking. Furthermore, it would appear 'that the Council has set its seal of approval on what the Court of Justice has done so far in interpreting the scope of the Directive, and has left further consideration of this "hot potato" in the hands of the court'. The EU Council of Ministers has missed an opportunity to offer a guide through this particular legal maze. One possible – and preferable – option would have been to adopt the recommendation of the British House of Lords Select Committee on the European Communities (5th Report, Session

1995–96, para. 32), as discussed in Chapters 4 and 5, that the Directive should give a non-exhaustive list of matters to be taken into account in determining the applicability of the Directive in a particular case without any presumption that the Directive does not apply if one or more of the factors is not present. All the facts and circumstances of the case should be taken into account.

Further problems may be caused by the Amended Directive's exclusion from the scope of the ARD of 'an administrative reorganisation of public administrative authorities, or the transfer of administrative functions between public administrative authorities' (Article 1(1)(c)). This follows the earlier decision of the ECJ in *Henke* (1996) that the Directive did not apply in such circumstances. It is hard to see how such an approach gives effect to the Directive's principal purpose of employment protection. It is maintained that a preferable view was that adopted by the Advocate General in *Henke* where he stated that the Directive was applicable 'whenever employees within the meaning of the national protective provisions are employed in an undertaking or an organisational entity'. As the British TUC pointed out, the ECJ's approach would have posed particular difficulties in Britain during the recent reorganisation of local government, where it was generally assumed throughout that process that the ARD and the domestic regulations were applicable: 'Had Henke been decided earlier, there would have been no guarantee of protection for the thousands of workers affected by reorganisation who would have lost their continuity of employment and other acquired rights.'

Insolvency transfers within the EU?

The Amended Directive effects the most significant changes in relation to transfers by insolvent transferors. The original Directive was silent on the question of its applicability in insolvency situations and so it has been left to the jurisprudence of the ECJ to set out the parameters. The ECJ has ruled in *Abels* (1985) that that the ARD does not apply to transfers in the context of liquidation proceedings, but that it does apply to proceedings short of liquidation aimed at ensuring the continuance of the business, while the Amended Directive permits EU member states to exclude the application of the Directive in cases where the undertaking, business or part of the business being transferred 'is the subject of bankruptcy proceedings or any analogous insolvency proceedings which have been instituted with a view to the liquidation of the assets of the transferor and are under the supervision of a competent public authority'. This adoption of the distinction drawn in the earlier case law between the liquidation of insolvent companies and other ways of dealing with them, e.g. the appointment of an administrator by the court, can be subjected to a number of criticisms. The difficulty with this distinction is that it focuses on the ultimate fate of the transferor rather than on the position of the employees and the transferee when the viable parts of the business are sold, something that is a central feature of any procedure for handling redundancies, whether through liquidation or otherwise. The distinction is inconsistent with the ARD's aims of employment protection, providing insolvency practitioners with a positive incentive to adopt the liquidation route as opposed to putting together a 'rescue package' for insolvent employees, and is likely to lead to considerable litigation. As the TUC has pointed out, 'the reality is that it will not always be clear at the outset of the procedure whether it will lead to a continuation of the business or its termination'. It is submitted that the correct approach to the problem was adopted by the ECJ in the recent case of *Jules Dethier* (1998). Here, the court held that the correct criterion to apply for the application of the Directive was not the purpose of the liquidation proceedings (i.e. the realisation of the assets of the company) but whether the company continued to trade after the liquidation process was initiated. This is a far superior test for determining the applicability of the Directive but it is questionable whether it can outlive the formula adopted by the Amended Directive.

In the context of proceedings short of liquidation such as administration or judicial arrangements, often termed 'pre-insolvency matters', instituted with a view to securing the survival of the undertaking, the amended ARD provides that EU member states will have a discretion to provide that the transferor's debts, either in the form of arrears of payments, damages or other liabilities, due before the business transfer or prior to the opening of insolvency proceedings, do not transfer to the transferee. This amendment can be relied upon only if the affected employees are afforded the protection required by the EC 'Insolvency' Directive 80/897/EEC, whereby some of the employees' claims, unmet by the transferor and now not claimable against the transferee, are paid out of a government-financed guarantee fund.

In addition or instead, under Article 4(A)(2) of the Amended Directive EU member states can opt to allow the employer and employee representatives to 'agree alterations to the employees' terms and conditions of employment designed to safeguard employment opportunities by ensuring the survival of the undertaking, business or part of the undertaking or business'. This provision represents a modification of the principle of the compulsory transfer of employment on the employees' existing terms and conditions where there is collective agreement: a modification firmly rejected by both the British and European courts.

European trade unions were very critical of the proposals in the earlier initial draft to enable 'employee representatives' to negotiate pay cuts or reductions in conditions of employment in order to ensure the survival of the undertaking. The second draft did contain a proviso to seek to meet this concern requiring that the employee representatives should 'enjoy sufficient independence to carry out the functions assigned to them' but this was omitted from the text which was finally adopted. Even had this proviso had been included in the final text, it would not have fully assuaged the unions' concern:

> The Directive already permits dismissals for 'economic, technical or organisational reasons' and this gives employers a high level of flexibility in crisis situations. Unions will be placed in an invidious position if they are told that unless they agree to certain changes the business will fail. Article 4(A)(2) is an additional and unnecessary device that could be used by unscrupulous employers to try and reduce labour costs and employees' contractual rights when this might not be strictly necessary.

As an attempted response to such concerns, Article 4(A)(4) of the Amended Directive states that 'Member States shall take appropriate measures with a view to preventing misuse of insolvency proceedings in such a way as to deprive employees of the rights provided for in this Directive.' How such a provision can be given effective practical application is a matter for serious conjecture.

More information and consultation rights!

These requirements are little changed, though the amendment brings the information and consultation requirements in line with the equivalent provisions of the Collective Redundancies Directive. As a result, it will be no defence for the employer to argue that the actions or omissions of a parent company excuse a failure to inform and consult (Article 6(4)). Also, the consultation and information requirements to individual employees apply where, through no fault of their own, there are no representatives to be informed or consulted (Article 6). As noted in Chapter 5, the new 1999 Consultation Regulations did much to modify the UK law on consultation, repealing the 1995 Regulations and bringing consultation and information rights into compliance with the original Directive.

A lost opportunity?

As can be seen from the Amended Directive, provision may be made for collectively agreed variation of terms and conditions in an insolvency situation in order to ensure the survival of the undertaking. However, the EU Commission did not take the opportunity to give more general application to this principle and extend it beyond insolvency cases. For instance, the scope for transferee employers to seek an agreed variation of the terms and conditions of employment of transferred employees has been addressed in a number of European and domestic cases. The UK's highest court, the House of Lords, in its recent judgment in *Wilson and others* v *St Helens Borough Council/British Fuels Ltd* v. *Meade and Baxendale* confirmed, in line with the ECJ authorities, that if employees are transferred on a relevant transfer of undertaking their terms and conditions cannot lawfully be varied for a reason connected to the transfer, regardless of whether they consent to the variations and regardless of how long after the transfer they are made. However, Lord Slynn, giving the main judgment, did express the view that 'there must, or at least may, come a time when the link with the transfer is broken or can be treated as no longer effective.' In such circumstances an agreed variation could be valid.

It is disappointing that good employers across the EU who seek to agree changes in terms and conditions of employment with their workforce will find that any agreed variation is invalid if the change is prompted by the transfer. What underlies the 'no waiver' principle is the difficulties in determining whether or not a particular agreement is truly based on the consent of the workers affected. This certainly may be a legitimate concern where employees do not have recourse to trade union representation but less so where a trade union is recognised and there are established collective bargaining arrangements. There is a contradiction between the 'no waiver' principle and the consultation requirements laid down by the ARD. There is little point in engaging in consultation with employee representatives about the consequences of a transfer if an agreement to vary terms and conditions which is the outcome of the consultative process is null and void. Moreover, as Rubenstein, commenting on the EAT stage in *Wilson*, observes: 'The decision also creates the paradox that a transferee needing to reduce costs is protected by TUPE if it dismisses employees on the grounds of redundancy, but is precluded from offering to save jobs if costs can be reduced by varying contractual terms' (see IRLR commentary).

Moreover, in terms of the proposed inclusion of share transfers, the British House of Lords Select Committee, with the support of trade unions and despite opposition from employers, recommended that takeovers by transfer should be brought within the scope of the Directive. In 1974, the original proposal for the Acquired Rights Directive encompassed share transfer cases but following negotiations its scope was narrowed. Share transfer was and remains the most frequent mechanism for takeovers in the UK and although there is no change in the legal personality of the employer, it may have as serious consequences for employees as business transfers carried through by other means. The UK government did not support the Select Committees's proposal and the EU Commission did not propose extending the scope of the law to cover share transfers in any of its drafts of the Amended Directive.

Another omitted proposal is that relating to joint liability. The original Directive offered EU member states a choice as to whether to introduce joint liability between transferor and transferee in respect of obligations which arise from an employment contract. While a number of EU member states have adopted some form of joint liability, this option has not been taken up by the UK. Under the initial draft amendment it would have been mandatory for the transferor and transferee to be jointly liable for debts falling due for up to a year after that date. In its second draft proposal the EU

Commission wished to retain mandatory joint and several liability for all obligations falling due *before* the date of transfer. From a trade union perspective, 'employees have a legitimate expectation that debts unpaid by an insolvent transferor can be recovered from a solvent transferee'. However, the UK government made it clear that it proposed to oppose any amendment which would impose mandatory joint and several liability. It took the view that other EU member states would be unlikely to support the EU Commission's proposal and that the issue should be dealt with under national law and practice. This stance ultimately won the day and EU member states are left with the option of imposing joint and several liability (see Article 3(1)).

Most disappointingly for employees is the fact that the new Directive does not resolve the long-standing legal debate relating to the transferability of pension rights post-transfer, particularly where in *Barber* v. *GRE* (1990) the ECJ ruled that pensions were pay and pay is transferred under the ARD. Under the amending Directive, supplementary occupational pension schemes are excluded from the automatic transfer of contractual rights under both the ARD and TUPE (Regulation 7). Under the amended Directive occupational pension schemes continue to be excluded from automatic transfer 'unless Member States provide otherwise'. The addition of this phrase serves no legal purpose since Article 7 already allows EU member states 'to introduce laws, regulations and administrative provisions more favourable to employees than those set out in the Directive'. Indeed, eight EU member states have already legislated to provide for the transfer of occupational schemes in defined circumstances. The reason for this legally pointless amendment may well have been to provide those EU member states who wish to legislate for the automatic transfer of pension rights an additional political justification for doing so.

As noted in Chapter 4, the British House of Lords Select Committee recommended that consideration should be given by the EU Commission to the inclusion in the Directive of a requirement that the transferee should be obliged to provide 'comparable' as opposed to identical pension rights to transferred employees. It was thought that, given the wide diversity in the nature, contribution levels and benefits provided by occupational pension schemes, it would not be practicable for employees to remain in their existing schemes following a transfer. The exclusion of the automatic transfer of pension rights – or comparable rights – creates an anomaly in a situation where other contractual rights transfer. It has now been clearly recognised in a series of cases dealing with the scope of Article 141 of the EU Treaty that pensions are a form of deferred pay and, therefore, there is no logical reason why they should not be dealt with in the same way as other conditions of employment relating to remuneration. In the UK, it is already the policy for public sector contractors contracting out work to the private sector in a TUPE transfer to require the transferees to provide broadly comparable occupational provision or adequate compensation to transferring employees for any loss of pension right, and even without a suitable amendment to the Directive, the UK should legislate to make it a statutory obligation for transferees to provide pension benefits that are commensurate with those provided by the transferor.

The Amended Directive (98/50/EC) does little to advance the cause of employment protection in the context of business transfers.

In relation to insolvent business transfers the Directive gives EU member states a wide degree of discretion in terms of the type and strength of protection they will offer. On other matters such as pension rights and share transfers no progress has been made. A golden opportunity was missed to 'nail down' a clear definition of what constitutes a transfer of a business. Consequently, we are left with a whole series of confusing and contradictory rulings from the European Court of Justice which provide little or no EU-wide guidance to HR practitioners, trade union officials and lawyers but which offer the unscrupulous transferee employer generous scope for avoidance of obligations to the transferor's workforce.

The future of contracting-out and TUPE

As observed in Chapter 4 the ETO defences will in the future challenge business transfers consequential from contracting-out scenarios. As a result it is clear that in the future these defences will have to be clarified either by the ECJ or the UK courts/tribunals. As stated in Chapter 4, adopting a purposive approach towards the construction of Regulation 8 will be the way forward. For instance, Mummery LJ stated in *Trafford* v. *Sharpe* (1994) that:

> The rights of workers must be safeguarded 'so far as possible'. It is not always possible to safeguard the rights of workers. As is recognised...the rights of workers not to be dismissed on the transfer of an undertaking must not stand in the way of dismissals which take place for economic reasons entailing changes in the workforce. In such cases the rights of workers may be outweighed by the economic reasons.

Such a comment blatantly asserts that the ARD no longer safeguards the employee first and foremost; instead the primary objective of the ARD is subject to a weighing up of the employer's economic situation against the employee's livelihood. Such a decision sends out two clear messages to all those involved in business transfers: firstly, that employers should not avoid TUPE; and secondly, that the ETO defences provide boundaries from which employers and employees can negotiate changes post-transfer. Evidently, the future of 'best value' or contracting-out generally will rely upon applying TUPE and then utilising the ETO defences and collective bargaining to bring about change in order to sustain the business into the future.

Revising the TUPE Regulations 2001

Following a two-year silence since the 1999 consultation on TUPE and redundancy the UK government is to undertake a short consultation on the draft revised TUPE Regulations as a consequence of the 1998 Amended Directive.

The text of the Amended Directive is interesting in that it can be seen, as discussed above, both as bringing the text into line with the growing case law of the ECJ and as an attempt to address the diverse concerns of the EU member states about business transfers. The amended ARD remains one of partial harmonisation, which provides member states with an option both to increase employee protection directly and to facilitate the preservation of employment opportunities indirectly by affording a facility to adapt terms and conditions. The amendments to the ARD are therefore consistent with the principle of subsidiarity, i.e. the ability to execute at the domestic level what is most practical to do so at this level, and respect for national practices. To that end the revised TUPE Regulations must bridge the gap between meeting the demands of national practices with the need to fully comply with the newly Amended ARD, so as to avoid *Francovich* actions as considered in Chapter 5.

In brief, what proposed changes we are likely to see is not known at present. However, at the time of writing we can speculate that the following issues are likely to be addressed in the forthcoming public consultation.

Definition of a 'TUPE transfer'

As noted in the discussion of the amended ARD above, revised Regulation 1 is likely to follow the 1998 ARD's lead and provide a clearer definition than the previous version, but is expected to clearly rule contracting-out transfers within the ambit of the Directive. Nothing too radical is anticipated here, except a full adherence to the guidance, albeit with variations, from the ECJ.

Inclusion of comparable pensions

Contrary to both existing Regulation 7 and the 1998 ARD's amendment, it is believed that the DTI is keen to include pension rights within the newly revised TUPE framework. The rationale for such is purely based upon moral grounds rather than legal, albeit that the government was not happy with the outcomes in the *Walden Engineering* v. *Warrener* and *Adams* v. *Lancashire CC* (1996) cases, where pensions were non-transferable. Consequently, a compromise is expected, where employers do not have to transfer existing occupational pensions but can provide 'comparable' pensions. Notice that the term 'equivalent' is not operative here.

Inclusion of 'sea-going vessels'

A long-standing omission, it is promised, will be rectified by the revised TUPE Regulations, namely that sea-going vessels will be brought within the scope of TUPE.

Determining TUPE's application

It is believed that the DTI is concerned about consistency in approaching TUPE cases within the UK and that it is proposing to question how such consistency might be attained. It follows that ETs will perhaps be given extra powers in this respect, for example that a directions-style hearing mechanism will be introduced whereby, before TUPE cases proceed, a determination of its application will be considered.

However, Article 6 (Right to a Fair Hearing) of the 1950 European Convention on Human Rights, implemented under the 1998 Human Rights Act, may be problematical for such a proposal, since it could be argued that such an approach might prejudice the future hearing, having applied TUPE or not. In any event, the alternative would be a TUPE 'tsar', where a newly created body would deal solely with TUPE cases. The consequences are unimaginable! Whatever the outcome, the government's attention to consistency is well intended since, given the state of the current law, consistency would help achieve the much needed clarity.

Sanctions for non-compliance

What is clear from the 1998 Amended Directive is the fact that sanctions are to be imposed for non-compliance. This we have already experienced in the UK in terms of consultation and information (13 weeks' pay compensation for non-consultation). While the newly inserted Articles 7A and 7B of the 1998 ARD spell out sanctions for discrimination and avoidance, how the revised TUPE Regulations implement this will be worth looking out for. How will it be accomplished and who will enforce it? the courts/tribunals?

Consultation rights

Following the lead of the 1998 ARD the revised TUPE Regulations are expected to clarify the duty to inform and consult. This will have little effect on current UK practice given the prescriptive and useful nature of the 1999 Consultation Regulations.

Outstanding issues

As with the 1998 ARD what is likely to be omitted from the revised TUPE Regulations is a clear position on contracting-out (or perhaps the revised scope in Regulation 1 will resolve this issue). Most certainly, as it is discretionary, joint liability will be omitted. In addition, the inclusion of share and insolvency transfers will continue in accordance with the provisions of the Amended Directive. Moreover, it would be very unlikely if the ETO defences were to be clarified, given the UK government's position that they have already provided guidance on them and that this is a matter for the courts/tribunals, given the existing case law. Lastly, the revised TUPE Regulations are likely to ignore the issue of transnational transfers, suggesting that this is a matter which has little relevance in the UK or that the EWC legislation will handle cross-border EU/EEA business transfers.

The TUPE Regulations 2001 are due to be in force by July 2001. Exciting times lie ahead…

The legality of the revised TUPE Regulations

While claims against EU governments exist under the Francovich doctrine, any EU member state could have its transposition of its newly revised measures challenged in their domestic courts. Subject to s. 2(2) of the 1972 European Communities Act, the UK government's implementation of the amending 1998 ARD, in the terms of the revised TUPE Regulations, could be challenged in the British courts on the grounds of being *ultra vires*. Under Article 7 of the ARD, EU member states are reminded that the Directive only provides a minimum floor of rights and that EU member states can provide employees with more favourable rights should they so desire.

Clearly, the amended ARD incorporates several options under which EU member states are empowered to introduce provisions which are more favourable to employees, such as including pension rights or the capacity to vary terms in insolvency situations.

However, any provisions which could be construed as a reinterpretation of the ARD's minimum standards could open up the potentiality of litigation. To that end, it is anticipated that the revised TUPE Regulations will meet the minimum standards established under the amended ARD rather than adopt a more favourable approach, in order to avoid High Court actions for *ultra vires*/judicial review claims.

Summary

Evidently, although the Amended Directive is on the EU's statute book, the UK has yet to fully implement it (but the clock is ticking loudly!). Furthermore, the 1998 Amended Directive has all the hallmarks of a compromise document. However, some of the new TUPE proposals, if they come to fruition, bode well for clearer, more certain times ahead on some TUPE issues. On the other hand, should the revised TUPE Regulations 2001 remain a weak legal instrument, then uncertainty will remain and the need for business managers and lawyers to think TUPE before acting will become important in the future.

To sum up: the new ARD (1998) replaces the original 1977 Directive and by and large redefines a 'transfer' to reflect the immense amount of existing case law. The Directive, though, is still not applicable to insolvency situations. However, the Amended Directive allows for the possible transfer of pension rights. Consequently, the revised TUPE Regulations, due by July 2001, will replace the 1981 TUPE Regulations and should reinforce the 'minor' changes brought about by the 1998 Amended ARD. To that end the new Regulations define a 'TUPE transfer' (including contracting-out transfers) and include comparable pensions and 'sea-going vessels', as well as establish sanctions for non-compliance.

As for future business transfers, the key issues remain the scope of the law (case law needs clarification), consultation, pensions and sanctions. Other outstanding issues are the position of contracting-out, joint liability, the non-inclusion of share transfers, insolvency transfers and ETO defences. These need clarity. As ECJ rulings continue and more transnational transfers occur within the EU, the EU institutions may in time become unhappy with the 1998 ARD and more reform will be necessary.

CHAPTER 8

Conclusions and future
strategies for TUPE

The starting point of this guide was the triumph of a determined Mrs Dines who, having fallen victim of a CCT business transfer, pursued her claim for TUPE protection before the national courts, relying upon EC law. Her case clearly demonstrated both the economic and legal consequences which can result from a simple business transfer from company A to company B, as well as the legal conflict between UK and EU laws.

This guide has shown that business transfers are commonplace within the EU employment environment today. While the ARD has facilitated market harmonisation, it has also given employment protection rights. The current debate's obsession with flexibility versus social rights must be resolved. The law needs to recognise that an economic decision taken by an employer, even a previous employer, can have devastating effects for individual employees. The rival views among UK employers and employees about the priorities raised within a TUPE business transfer must be remembered by lawyers and judges when dealing with business transfers.

Contracting-out has transformed and improved public services, but it has been demonstrated that it can dismantle statutory employment rights in the process. The ARD, albeit drafted in another era, has survived the changing economic environment of the EU through a process of legal interpretation and political horse-trading. The present legal framework does not provide for the transparency which all the contractual parties to a business transfer require and desire. In a discussion of the law relating to business transfers, the fact that a group of labour experts from all the EU member states designed the ARD in 1974 to encourage worker involvement in decision-making and provide for social protection within the workplace is a crucial starting point for the 1998 Amended Directive in the future.

The problem with EU law-making is that it is backward-looking. The EU Commission's Amended ARD only seeks to resolve old problems encountered by the Directive and neglects to be forward-looking and consider what future EU developments require of business transfers. As a consequence of this approach, the role of the ECJ is confined to one which modernises the law by way of clarification and extending the original intentions of a directive to meet the demands of those affected. The law relating to business transfers is a good illustration of this situation which faces EU policy-makers and lawyers. EU law-makers should therefore monitor the affects of legislation more often and enact change more readily, so that legislative frameworks are always tackling the problems of tomorrow rather than today. Alternatively, the legislative draftsbody of the EU, the EU Commission, should be more forward-looking in the first instance. As law is used to promote change, it should be forward-looking, whether at the domestic or EU level. Moreover, the history of the ARD prompts questions as to why EU laws are not directly applicable. The current reliance on 15 EU member states to fully implement Directives encourages those EU member states' governments who opposed the proposed law in the EU Council to attempt to evade the Directive or even weaken it during its transposition into domestic law, both these actions being contrary to EC law. However, these dangerous circumstances can prevail, as evidenced by the UK's treatment of TUPE explained throughout this guide.

Under the current law, UK employers' creative compliance subverts the original intention of the ARD. Creative compliance is concerned with the behaviour of individual firms. In particular, it is about how firms conform to the requirements of the law, but avoid the law's overall purpose. For example, what firms do to conform to the consultation requirements is to consult with their elected employees but then fail to 'seek agreement'. Much of the future debate surrounding business transfers is likely to centre on how to avoid TUPE litigation. According to some expert legal practitioners this can be done effectively by having agreements between the transferor and transferee which iron out many of the problems experienced. For instance, agreements are commonly reached on pensions, whether TUPE applies or not and establishing some core indemnities or business transfer guarantees which all the parties subjected to the business transfer have agreed and are aware of.

In this guide a consideration of the consequences of business transfers for the terms and conditions of employment, employment protection and employment policies has illustrated that EC–UK law conflicts, and that disagreement between employers' business interests and employees' contractual rights exists. As for the future of the law relating to business transfers, much further litigation can be expected while EU policy-makers debate the current concerns about competition and labour standards. The ARD and TUPE alike have acquired a bad reputation for their wide and unpredictable scope. The fact that the UK government belatedly transposed the ARD into English law and was slow in realising the importance of EU social policy has contributed to the current morass of legal complexity surrounding business transfers. In conclusion, even over twenty years after the introduction of the ARD, there still is a significant amount of uncertainty about the governance of business transfers.

The conflicting strategies on business transfers

The following sections summarise the strategies adopted by employers, trade unions, the government and the judiciary within the UK when dealing with business transfers.

Employer strategies

It is commonplace that in handling business transfers employers are more likely to be advised by external lawyers or consultants. This often means that the major aim of an employer's legal strategy is to interpret the law as it suits them. Unsure of the scope of the legislation and having received speculative advice based on uncertain law, employers have continued to pursue their own aims rather than following the general purpose of the law enshrined in the ARD and TUPE. It is clear that they have achieved this by arguing that certain transfers are not within the scope of the law. In the future, now that contracting-out (or not – see the latest Finnish case *Oy Liikenne Ab* (2001)) is generally within the scope of the ARD, UK employers hope that the ETO defences will prevent their plans being disrupted and preserve the economic aims of the contracting-out legislation.

Trade union strategies

With the current law being squarely posited in favour of safeguarding employees subjected to business transfers it might be assumed that the unions' strategy could not be more straightforward. In a UK context, the unions' strategy is one of making their members aware of the issues and their rights, supporting applicants where appropriate in tribunals and the courts, and seeking to enforce their rights to consultation where employers seek to ignore them. While the unions' strategy accepts that they cannot prevent contracting-out, it does recognise that they can be active in informing, consulting, representing and protecting their members, where possible, especially under the 1999 Regulations. UK unions are now understanding the need to insist on the transfer of existing or comparable pension provisions, and that collective agreements on pension provision can be vital as a means of securing existing pension rights. At the EU level, with a closer union between the UK TUC and ETUC, this confederation is seeking to support actions against those EU Member States who fail to implement the ARD adequately resulting in harm to EU workers. These Francovich actions may prove to be ineffectual unless state liability for the detriments incurred by workers can be proven.

Individual employees' strategies

As for individual 'employees' themselves, if they are not trade union members they should seek advice. They will be advised to either take up their right to object, which results in unemployment and is therefore a perilous path to follow, or alternatively to agree terms and conditions in their contracts in order to protect their employment. As the most exposed group, these workers cannot generally afford legal advice and therefore may not understand the law, nor what legal entitlements they hold. In such circumstances seeking advice from voluntary organisations is absolutely vital to these workers and an advisable strategy to follow.

UK government's strategy

As in all matters of employment law, the third party concerned is the state. Government can intercede between the parties and their respective interests. As with the unions' strategy, governmental strategy has two planes: the domestic and the EU. Both these strategies, however, seek to preserve perceived national interests. After initially refusing to include contracting-out business transfers within the scope of the ARD, the government has now advised UK employers to establish an ETO reason for their business transfer in order to defend any litigation which might arise. On TUPE matters, it would prefer to legislate itself, under the subsidiarity principle, rather than adhere to its EU obligations. In the full knowledge that such an application of the subsidiarity principle is not applicable, the UK government has sought to meet its Treaty and EU membership obligations by establishing the bare minimum which the ARD sets out and requires. The end result has been the inadequately drafted TUPE Regulations and a strategy which was partially successful, until its exposure in EU infraction proceedings.

Judicial strategies

Judges can either assist a government's policy or dismantle it. In the UK, while the judges have generally favoured the government's view, that has not always been the case, with the courts upholding employees' rights when subjected to business transfers following the ECJ's purposive rulings. The question arises whether this approach will end when it comes to the courts having to adjudicate on the ETO defences. As Chapter 4 has already suggested this change in strategy could mean a return to a situation like that in the 1970s, where judges under a similar set of defences termed 'some other substantial reason' (SOSR – now under s. 98, ERA 1996) enforced and legitimised managerial prerogative. The return to such an era, based around the ETO defences, would mean a revival in placing property rights above personal, employment rights in business transfers. Thus, we would witness a return to the common law seen in the UK prior to 1982, entrenched in their Lordships 1940 judgment in *Nokes*.

As with union and governmental strategies, judicial strategy also lies at two levels. At the EU level, the ECJ has clearly shown a strategy which places the purpose of the ARD at the peak of its reasoning. Such a purposive strategy can overturn domestic decisions. On the other hand, at the UK level judicial reasoning largely depends on the individual judge's frame of reference, as well as their understanding of EC law and appreciation of economics. These three factors determine the individual judge's point of view regarding business transfers.

Developing a legally compliant modern business strategy

It is clear that these differing strategies need to be reconciled in order to make the law relating to business transfers more transparent for all concerned. In response to these differing approaches a modern legal business strategy needs to be established.

Below are some useful checklists and an overall summary.

Starting point!

1.   All business transfers should operate under TUPE.

2.   Act fairly/'reasonably' at all times.

3.   Beware of restrictive covenants and existing practices.

Managing change

1. Seek consent from employees (note: *Wilson* case).

2. Notice and offer arrangements to all staff affected.

3. Contractual right to vary.

4. Incentive payments may be used.

5. Red circling of employees just may apply.

6. Establish ETO where necessary.

7. Beware of unfair dismissals.

Contracting-out transfers

1. Service must be an identifiable part and retain its identity for ARD/TUPE to apply.

2. TUPE applies even if service is performed for the former employer.

3. TUPE applies even when second generation and later contracting-out occurs.

Contracting-out and the law

1. *Suzen* – requires either a transfer of significant assets or labour-intensive situations (i.e. major part of the workforce).

2.   *Oy Liikenne* – requires a consideration of the type of undertaking and the transfer of the substantial assets in order to provide the service transferred (i.e. the transfer of labour alone is not sufficient for a transfer).

3.   *Solution* – enquire about activities pre-transfer, tangible and intangible assets; identify employees affected and their functions; and ask whether an economic entity will retain its identity post-transfer.

Negotiating transfers

1.   Assess bargaining position.

2.   Obtain financial guarantees.

3.   Consider joint liability issues.

4.   Due diligence is the key and *must* be carried out.

Indemnities?

1.   *Purchaser/buyer* – post-transfer liabilities; failure to provide information; costs of vendor dismissals.

2.   *Vendor/seller* – acts/omissions pre-transfer; failure to inform/consult; undisclosed employees affected.

Warranties?

1. Obtain an accurate disclosure letter.

2. Consider existing employment contracts/documentation.

3. Acquire information, documents and existing data on pay details/reviews/severance payments/pensions/bonuses.

4. Check for absent employees – sickness, maternity, secondment.

5. Ensure there is no litigation pending.

6. Enquire about collective agreements.

7. Ascertain any trade union recognition/arrangements.

8. Consider any transfer-connected dismissals.

9. Enquire about HSE/CRE/EOC/DRC/other external agency investigation.

Using warranties!

1. Ensure accuracy of information.

2. Qualify information/data – check it all.

3. Note any limitations.

Outline purchase agreement

1. Acknowledge TUPE.

2. Set out the date and time of transfer.

3. List affected employees.

4. Define each party's obligations under TUPE.

Consultation

1. Apply and undertake the obligations under the 1999 Consultation Regulations (from 1/11/1999).

2. Decide who is to be consulted – trade unions or elected representatives.

3. If elected reps, hold nominations and ballot(s).

4. Note that in the event of a failure to elect your obligations are fulfilled.

5. Remember your duties to inform and consult.

6. Always consult 'in good time', 'with a view to reaching agreement'.

7. Consult on *all* the legal, economic and social implications.

8. Note the rights of elected reps to facilities, access and information.

9. Always assure confidentiality throughout.

Rights and liabilities

1. Existing employment contracts.

2. Pre-existing terms and conditions, collective agreements.

3. Continuity of service.

4. Retention of employees.

5. Protection from dismissal (if related to the transfer).

Who transfers?

1. Employees.

2. Part of undertaking.

3. Absentees.

4. Except those objecting to transfer and dismissed unconnected with the transfer.

Pensions?

1. Occupational pension schemes do *not* transfer.

2. TUPE applies to individual or personal pension arrangements.

3. Accrued rights remain protected post-transfer.

4. Comparable or equivalent pension schemes can be offered but require agreement.

TUPE or not TUPE?

1. TUPE aims to protect the rights of employees.

2. Employment rights pass and continue.

3. Avoidance of TUPE is not condoned by the courts (cf. *ECM* v. *Cox*).

4. Good practice suggests that TUPE be applied.

5. Utilise consultation, agreement, collective bargaining, change methods and ETO where applicable.

Remedies

1. Employees can complain to an ET.

2. A declaration can be given.

3. Four to 13 weeks' pay compensation can be awarded.

4. Unfair dismissal claims (£51,600 maximum) can be awarded.

Closing point!

1. Be aware of the law.

2. Apply TUPE in all cases.

3. Execute obligations under TUPE.

4. Use/check warranties/indemnities.

5.   Undertake a due diligence exercise.

6.   Inform and consult those affected by the transfer.

7.   Act fairly at all times.

8.   Seek future business success…

TUPE in a nutshell

By way of summary, the Transfer of Undertakings (Protection of Employment) Regulations 1981 – TUPE – apply to business transfers. Where such business transfers take place all the pre-existing contracts of employment transfer automatically from the existing owner to the new owner. Subsequently, the new owner carries all the liabilities. Such business transfers exclude share sales, since no change of employer occurs, only a change in shareholders. Contracting-out exercises have long been thought as outside the scope of TUPE – it depends on whether the service post-transfer retains its identity. Much case law has disputed this point, including the need for a significant transfer of assets, both labour and material assets. Such a debate continues, except to say that contracting-out should be viewed as within the scope in order to avoid later legal difficulties. These TUPE Regulations were enacted to comply with the original 1977 Acquired Rights Directive (now the 1998 Amended Directive).

Under such business transfers, the employees employed by the seller who work in the part being transferred and are immediately employed before the transfer are transferred. On transfer, these workers' existing contracts, all associated rights, duties and liabilities, collective agreements and any statutory liabilities are transferred across, except for occupational pensions. Note that criminal liabilities do not transfer. The employer selling the business must inform and consult with either recognised trade unions or elected representatives in the absence of trade unions about the transfer. Such consultation should consider the legal, economic and social implications. Reasonable time should be given to undertake such obligations.

Any dismissal for a reason connected with the transfer will be deemed automatically unfair, unless for economic, technical or organisational purposes. A one-year qualifying period is required for all unfair dismissal claims. The ETO reasons have been considered in case law and government guidance has existed since 1991 on their applicability. The imposition of new terms and conditions will result in automatic unfair dismissal claims. Note the agreement to new terms and conditions may be ineffective if they are seen to be related to the transfer. Collective agreements transfer, but a new employer may not be bound by them and can withdraw from those agreements not incorporated into employees' contracts.

TUPE contains anti-avoidance provisions and similarly the UK courts view the evasion of TUPE as unlawful. To that end TUPE will be applied as a sanction in such cases.

Postscript

At the time of writing, the long awaited revised TUPE Regulations remain pending – these need to be implemented by July 2001. Watch this space for further developments… interesting times lie ahead.

'It's a story of doom and gloom about the costs of fighting a TUPE case…we are frightened' (Staffordshire University Survey, 1996). You should not be frightened now, and should be reassured that its not all doom and gloom!

Good luck. I hope this guide has simplified TUPE for you.

APPENDIX 1

Acquired Rights Directive 77/187 (Original Directive)

COUNCIL DIRECTIVE of 14 February 1977 on the approximation of the laws of the Member States relating to the safeguarding of employees' rights in the event of transfers of undertakings, businesses or parts of businesses (77/187/EEC)

THE COUNCIL OF THE EUROPEAN COMMUNITIES,

Having regard to the Treaty establishing the European Economic Community, and in particular Article 100 thereof,

Having regard to the proposal from the Commission,

Having regard to the opinion of the European Parliament,[1]

Having regard to the opinion of the Economic and Social Committee,[2]

---

1. *OJ* No. C95, 28.4.1975, p. 17.
2. *OJ* No. C255, 7.11.1975, p. 25.

Whereas economic trends are bringing in their wake, at both national and Community level, changes in the structure of undertakings, through transfers of undertakings, businesses or parts of businesses to other employers as a result of legal transfers or mergers;

Whereas it is necessary to provide for the protection of employees in the event of a change of employer, in particular, to ensure that their rights are safeguarded;

Whereas differences still remain in the Member States as regards the extent of the protection of employees in this respect and these differences should be reduced;

Whereas these differences can have a direct effect on the functioning of the common market;

Whereas it is therefore necessary to promote the approximation of laws in this field while maintaining the improvement described in Article 117 of the Treaty,

HAS ADOPTED THIS DIRECTIVE:

Section I Scope and definitions

Article 1

1.   This Directive shall apply to the transfer of an undertaking, business or part of a business to another employer as a result of a legal transfer or merger.

2.	This Directive shall apply where and in so far as the undertaking, business or part of the business to be transferred is situated within the territorial scope of the Treaty.

3.	This Directive shall not apply to sea-going vessels.

Article 2

For the purposes of this Directive:

(a)	'transferor' means any natural or legal person who, by reason of a transfer within the meaning of Article 1(1), ceases to be the employer in respect of the undertaking, business or part of the business;

(b)	'transferee' means any natural or legal person who, by reason of a transfer within the meaning of Article 1(1), becomes the employer in respect of the undertaking, business or part of the business;

(c)	'representatives of the employees' means the representatives of the employees provided for by the laws or practice of the Member States, with the exception of members of administrative, governing or supervisory bodies of companies who represent employees on such bodies in certain Member States.

Section II Safeguarding of employees' rights

Article 3

1.   The transferor's rights and obligations arising from a contract of employment or from an employment relationship existing on the date of a transfer within the meaning of Article 1(1) shall, by reason of such transfer, be transferred to the transferee. Member States may provide that, after the date of transfer within the meaning of Article 1(1) and in addition to the transferee, the transferor shall continue to be liable in respect of obligations which arose from a contract of employment or an employment relationship.

2.   Following the transfer within the meaning of Article 1(1), the transferee shall continue to observe the terms and conditions agreed in any collective agreement on the same terms applicable to the transferor under that agreement, until the date of termination or expiry of the collective agreement or the entry into force or application of another collective agreement. Member States may limit the period for observing such terms and conditions, with the provision that it shall not be less than one year.

3.   Paragraphs 1 and 2 shall not cover employees' rights to old-age, invalidity or survivors' benefits under supplementary company or inter-company pension schemes outside the statutory social security schemes in Member States. Member States shall adopt the measures necessary to protect the

interests of employees and of persons no longer employed in the transferor's business at the time of the transfer within the meaning of Article 1(1) in respect of rights conferring on them immediate or prospective entitlement to old-age benefits, including survivors' benefits, under supplementary schemes referred to in the first subparagraph.

Article 4

1. The transfer of an undertaking, business or part of a business shall not in itself constitute grounds for dismissal by the transferor or the transferee. This provision shall not stand in the way of dismissals that may take place for economic, technical or organizational reasons entailing changes in the workforce. Member States may provide that the first subparagraph shall not apply to certain specific categories of employees who are not covered by the laws or practice of the Member States in respect of protection against dismissal.

2. If the contract of employment or the employment relationship is terminated because the transfer within the meaning of Article 1(1) involves a substantial change in working conditions to the detriment of the employee, the employer shall be regarded as having been responsible for termination of the contract of employment or of the employment relationship.

Article 5

1. If the business preserves its autonomy, the status and function, as laid down by the laws, regulations or administrative provisions of the Member States, of the representatives or of the representation of the employees affected by the transfer within the meaning of Article 1(1) shall be preserved. The first subparagraph shall not apply if, under the laws, regulations, administrative provisions or practice of the Member States, the conditions necessary for the reappointment of the representatives of the employees or for the reconstitution of the representation of the employees are fulfilled.

2. If the term of office of the representatives of the employees affected by a transfer within the meaning of Article 1(1) expires as a result of the transfer, the representatives shall continue to enjoy the protection provided by the laws, regulations, administrative provisions or practice of the Member States.

Section III Information and consultation

Article 6

1. The transferor and the transferee shall be required to inform the representatives of their respective employees affected by a transfer within the meaning of Article 1(1) of the following:

-     the reasons for the transfer,

-     the legal, economic and social implications of the transfer for the employees,

-     measures envisaged in relation to the employees.

The transferor must give such information to the representatives of his employees in good time before the transfer is carried out.

The transferee must give such information to the representatives of his employees in good time, and in any event before his employees are directly affected by the transfer as regards their conditions of work and employment.

2.   If the transferor or the transferee envisages measures in relation to his employees, he shall consult his representatives of the employees in good time on such measures with a view to seeking agreement.

3.   Member States whose laws, regulations or administrative provisions provide that representatives of the employees may have recourse to an arbitration board to obtain a decision on the measures to be taken in relation to employees may limit the obligations laid down in paragraphs 1 and 2 to cases where the transfer carried out gives rise to a change in the business likely to entail serious disadvantages for a considerable number of the employees.

The information and consultations shall cover at least the measures envisaged in relation to the employees.

The information must be provided and consultations take place in good time before the change in the business as referred to in the first subparagraph is effected.

4. Member States may limit the obligations laid down in paragraphs 1, 2 and 3 to undertakings or businesses which, in respect of the number of employees, fulfil the conditions for the election or designation of a collegiate body representing the employees.

5. Member States may provide that where there are no representatives of the employees in an undertaking or business, the employees concerned must be informed in advance when a transfer within the meaning of Article 1(1) is about to take place.

Section IV Final provisions

Article 7

This Directive shall not affect the right of Member States to apply or introduce laws, regulations or administrative provisions which are more favourable to employees.

Article 8

1. Member States shall bring into force the laws, regulations and administrative provisions needed to comply with this Directive within two years of its notification and shall forthwith inform the Commission thereof.

2. Member States shall communicate to the Commission the texts of the laws, regulations and administrative provisions which they adopt in the field covered by this Directive.

Article 9

Within two years following expiry of the two-year period laid down in Article 8, Member States shall forward all relevant information to the Commission in order to enable it to draw up a report on the application of this Directive for submission to the Council.

Article 10

This Directive is addressed to the Member States.

Done at Brussels, 14 February 1977.
For the Council
The President
J. SILKIN

APPENDIX 2

Transfer of Undertakings (Protection of Employment) Regulations 1981/1794

Made: December 14, 1981

In-force date: February 1, 1982

These Regulations implement Council Directive No. 77/187/EEC.

Regulations 1 to 3 and 10 to 13 come into operation on 1st February 1982 and Regulations 4 to 9 and 14 on 1st May 1982. The principal provisions of the Regulations are as follows:

(a)   The Regulations apply where a person transfers a commercial undertaking or part thereof to another person (Regulation 3).

(b)   Such a transfer will not operate to terminate the employees' contracts of employment but any such contract which would otherwise have been terminated by the transfer will continue as if made between the transferee and the employees (Regulation 5). Provision is made for the continuance of collective agreements (Regulation 6). Regulations 5 and 6 do not apply to occupational pension schemes (Regulation 7).

(c)   Provision is made for the application of the remedies for unfair dismissal contained in the existing law where an employee of the transferor or transferee is dismissed by reason of the transfer (Regulation 8).

(d)   A trade union recognised by the transferor is deemed after a transfer to be similarly recognised by the transferee (Regulation 9).

(e)   The representatives of the employees who may be affected by the transfer are to be informed by the transferor and the transferee of the date of and the reasons for the transfer and its implications for them. Where the transferor or the transferee envisages that he will be taking measures in relation to the affected employees, he must enter into consultation with the said representatives (Regulation 10). A complaint may be presented to an industrial tribunal that these duties have not been performed and the tribunal may award compensation (Regulation 11).

Regulation 1 Citation, commencement and extent

(1)   These Regulations may be cited as the Transfer of Undertakings (Protection of Employment) Regulations 1981.

(2)   These Regulations, except Regulations 4 to 9 and 14, shall come into operation on 1st February 1982 and Regulations 4 to 9 and 14 shall come into operation on 1st May 1982.

(3)   These Regulations, except Regulations 11(10) and 13(3) and (4), extend to Northern Ireland.

Regulation 2 Interpretation

(1)   In these Regulations –
'collective agreement', 'employers' association', and 'trade union' have the same meanings respectively as in the 1974 Act or, in Northern Ireland, the 1976 Order;
'collective bargaining' has the same meaning as it has in the 1975 Act or, in Northern Ireland, the 1976 Order;
'contract of employment' means any agreement between an employee and his employer determining the terms and conditions of his employment;
'employee' means any individual who works for another person whether under a contract of service or apprenticeship or otherwise but does not include anyone who provides services under a contract for services and references to a person's employer shall be construed accordingly;

'the 1974 Act', 'the 1975 Act', 'the 1978 Act' and 'the 1976 Order' mean, respectively, the Trade Union and Labour Relations Act 1974, the Employment Protection Act 1975, the Employment Protection (Consolidation) Act 1978 and the Industrial Relations (Northern Ireland) Order 1976;

'recognised', in relation to a trade union, means recognised to any extent by an employer, or two or more associated employers (within the meaning of the 1978 Act, or, in Northern Ireland, the 1976 Order), for the purpose of collective bargaining;

'relevant transfer' means a transfer to which these Regulations apply and 'transferor' and 'transferee' shall be construed accordingly; and

'undertaking' includes any trade or business [...]

(2) References in these Regulations to the transfer of part of an undertaking are references to a transfer of a part which is being transferred as a business and, accordingly, do not include references to a transfer of a ship.

(3) For the purposes of these Regulations the representative of a trade union recognised by an employer is an official or other person authorised to carry on collective bargaining with that employer by that union.

Regulation 3 A relevant transfer

(1)   Subject to the provisions of these Regulations, these Regulations apply to a transfer from one person to another of an undertaking situated immediately before the transfer in the United Kingdom or a part of one which is so situated.

(2)   Subject as aforesaid, these Regulations so apply whether the transfer is effected by sale or by some other disposition or by operation of law.

(3)   Subject as aforesaid, these Regulations so apply notwithstanding –

   (a)   that the transfer is governed or effected by the law of a country or territory outside the United Kingdom;

   (b)   that persons employed in the undertaking or part transferred ordinarily work outside the United Kingdom;

   (c)   that the employment of any of those persons is governed by any such law.

(4)   It is hereby declared that a transfer of an undertaking or part of [one –]

   (a)   may be effected by a series of two or more transactions; and

   (b)   may take place whether or not any property is transferred to the transferee by the transferor.

(5) Where, in consequence (whether directly or indirectly) of the transfer of an undertaking or part of one which was situated immediately before the transfer in the United Kingdom, a ship within the meaning of the Merchant Shipping Act 1894 registered in the United Kingdom ceases to be so registered, these Regulations shall not affect the right conferred by section 5 of the Merchant Shipping Act 1970 (right of seamen to be discharged when ship ceases to be registered in the United Kingdom) on a seaman employed in the ship.

Regulation 4 Transfers by receivers and liquidators

(1) Where the receiver of the property or part of the property of a company or, in the case of a creditors' voluntary winding up, the liquidator of a company [or the administrator of a company appointed under Part II of the Insolvency Act 1986] transfers the company's undertaking, or part of the company's undertaking (the 'relevant undertaking') to a wholly owned subsidiary of the company, the transfer shall for the purposes of these Regulations be deemed not to have been effected until immediately before –

(a) the transferee company ceases (otherwise than by reason of its being wound up) to be a wholly owned subsidiary of the transferor company; or

(b) the relevant undertaking is transferred by the transferee company to another person; whichever first occurs, and, for the purposes of these Regulations, the transfer of the relevant undertaking shall be taken to have been effected immediately before that date by one transaction only.

(2)   In this Regulation –

'creditors' voluntary winding up' has the same meaning as in the Companies Act 1948 or, in Northern Ireland, the Companies Act (Northern Ireland) 1960; and 'wholly owned subsidiary' has the same meaning as it has for the purposes of section 150 of the Companies Act 1948 and section 144 of the Companies Act (Northern Ireland) 1960.

Regulation 5 Effect of relevant transfer on contracts of employment, etc.

(1)   Except where objection is made under paragraph (4A) below, a relevant transfer shall not operate so as to terminate the contract of employment of any person employed by the transferor in the undertaking or part transferred but any such contract which would otherwise have been terminated by the transfer shall have effect after the transfer as if originally made between the person so employed and the transferee.

(2)   Without prejudice to paragraph (1) above but subject to paragraph (4A) below, on the completion of a relevant transfer –

(a)   all the transferor's rights, powers, duties and liabilities under or in connection with any such contract, shall be transferred by virtue of this Regulation to the transferee; and

(b) anything done before the transfer is completed by or in relation to the transferor in respect of that contract or a person employed in that undertaking or part shall be deemed to have been done by or in relation to the transferee.

(3) Any reference in paragraph (1) or (2) above to a person employed in an undertaking or part of one transferred by a relevant transfer is a reference to a person so employed immediately before the transfer, including, where the transfer is effected by a series of two or more transactions, a person so employed immediately before any of those transactions.

(4) Paragraph (2) above shall not transfer or otherwise affect the liability of any person to be prosecuted for, convicted of and sentenced for any offence.

(4A) Paragraphs (1) and (2) above shall not operate to transfer his contract of employment and the rights, powers, duties and liabilities under or in connection with it if the employee informs the transferor or the transferee that he objects to becoming employed by the transferee.

(4B) Where an employee so objects the transfer of the undertaking or part in which he is employed shall operate so as to terminate his contract of employment with the transferor but he shall not be treated, for any purpose, as having been dismissed by the transferor.

(5)   [Paragraphs (1) and (4A) above are without prejudice to any right of an employee arising apart from these Regulations to terminate his contract of employment without notice if a substantial change is made in his working conditions to his detriment; but no such right shall arise by reason only that, under that paragraph, the identity of his employer changes unless the employee shows that, in all the circumstances, the change is a significant change and is to his detriment.

Regulation 6 Effect of relevant transfer on collective agreements

Where at the time of a relevant transfer there exists a collective agreement made by or on behalf of the transferor with a trade union recognised by the transferor in respect of any employee whose contract of employment is preserved by Regulation 5(1) above, then –

(a)   without prejudice to section 18 of the 1974 Act or Article 63 of the 1976 Order (collective agreements presumed to be unenforceable in specified circumstances) that agreement, in its application in relation to the employee, shall, after the transfer, have effect as if made by or on behalf of the transferee with that trade union, and accordingly anything done under or in connection with it, in its application as aforesaid, by or in relation to the transferor before the transfer, shall, after the transfer, be deemed to have been done by or in relation to the transferee; and

(b) any order made in respect of that agreement, in its application in relation to the employee, shall, after the transfer, have effect as if the transferee were a party to the agreement.

Regulation 7 Exclusion of occupational pensions schemes

(1) Regulations 5 and 6 above shall not apply –

    (a) to so much of a contract of employment or collective agreement as relates to an occupational pension scheme within the meaning of the Social Security Pensions Act 1975 or the Social Security Pensions (Northern Ireland) Order 1975; or

    (b) to any rights, powers, duties or liabilities under or in connection with any such contract or subsisting by virtue of any such agreement and relating to such a scheme or otherwise arising in connection with that person's employment and relating to such a scheme.

(2) For the purposes of paragraph (1) above any provisions of an occupational pension scheme which do not relate to benefits for old age, invalidity or survivors shall be treated as not being part of the scheme.

Regulation 8 Dismissal of employee because of relevant transfer

(1) Where either before or after a relevant transfer, any employee of the transferor or transferee is dismissed, that employee shall be treated for the purposes of Part V of the 1978 Act and Articles 20 to 41 of the 1976 Order (unfair dismissal) as unfairly dismissed if the transfer or a reason connected with it is the reason or principal reason for his dismissal.

(2) Where an economic, technical or organisational reason entailing changes in the workforce of either the transferor or the transferee before or after a relevant transfer is the reason or principal reason for dismissing an employee –

    (a) paragraph (1) above shall not apply to his dismissal; but

    (b) without prejudice to the application of section 57(3) of the 1978 Act or Article 22(10) of the 1976 Order (test of fair dismissal), the dismissal shall for the purposes of section 57(1)(b) of that Act and Article 22(1)(b) of that Order (substantial reason for dismissal) be regarded as having been for a substantial reason of a kind such as to justify the dismissal of an employee holding the position which that employee held.

(3) The provisions of this Regulation apply whether or not the employee in question is employed in the undertaking or part of the undertaking transferred or to be transferred.

(4)   Paragraph (1) above shall not apply in relation to the dismissal of any employee which was required by reason of the application of section 5 of the Aliens Restriction (Amendment) Act 1919 to his employment.

(5)   Paragraph (1) above shall not apply in relation to a dismissal of an employee if –

    (a)   the application of section 54 of the 1978 Act to the dismissal of the employee is excluded by or under any provision of Part V or sections 141 to 149 of the 1978 Act or of section 237 or 238 of the Trade Union and Labour Relations (Consolidation) Act 1992; or

    (b)   the application of Article 20 of the 1976 Order to the dismissal of the employee is excluded by or under any provision of Part III or Article 76 of that Order.

Regulation 9 Effect of relevant transfer on trade union recognition

(1)   This Regulation applies where after a relevant transfer the undertaking or part of the undertaking transferred maintains an identity distinct from the remainder of the transferee's undertaking.

(2)   Where before such a transfer an independent trade union is recognised to any extent by the transferor in respect of employees of any description who in consequence of the transfer become employees of the transferee, then, after the transfer –

(a)   the union shall be deemed to have been recognised by the transferee to the same extent in respect of employees of that description so employed; and

(b)   any agreement for recognition may be varied or rescinded accordingly.

Regulation 10   Duty to inform and consult representatives

(1)   In this Regulation and Regulation 11 below references to affected employees, in relation to a relevant transfer, are to any employees of the transferor or the transferee (whether or not employed in the undertaking or the part of the undertaking to be transferred) who may be affected by the transfer or may be affected by measures taken in connection with it; and references to the employer shall be construed accordingly.

(2)   Long enough before a relevant transfer to enable the employer of any affected employees to consult all the persons who are appropriate representatives of any of those affected employees, the employer shall inform those representatives of –

(a)   the fact that the relevant transfer is to take place, when, approximately, it is to take place and the reasons for it; and

(b)   the legal, economic and social implications of the transfer for the affected employees; and

(c)   the measures which he envisages he will, in connection with the transfer, take in relation to those employees or, if he envisages that no measures will be so taken, that fact; and

(d)   if the employer is the transferor, the measures which the transferee envisages he will, in connection with the transfer, take in relation to such of those employees as, by virtue of Regulation 5 above, become employees of the transferee after the transfer or, if he envisages that no measures will be so taken, that fact.

(2A) For the purposes of this Regulation the appropriate representatives of any employees are –

(a)   if the employees are of a description in respect of which an independent trade union is recognised by their employer, representatives of the trade union, or

(b)   in any other case, whichever of the following employee representatives the employer chooses:–

(i)   employee representatives appointed or elected by the affected employees otherwise than for the purposes of this Regulation, who (having regard to the purposes for and the method by which they were appointed or elected) have authority from those employees to receive information and to be consulted about [the transfer] on their behalf;

> (ii) employee representatives elected by them, for the purposes of this Regulation, in an election satisfying the requirements of Regulation 10A(1).

(3) The transferee shall give the transferor such information at such a time as will enable the transferor to perform the duty imposed on him by virtue of paragraph (2)(d) above.

(4) The information which is to be given to the appropriate representatives shall be given to each of them by being delivered to them, or sent by post to an address notified by them to the employer, or (in the case of representatives of a trade union) sent by post to the union at the address of its head or main office.

(5) Where an employer of any affected employees envisages that he will, in connection with the transfer, be taking measures in relation to any such employees he shall consult all the persons who are appropriate representatives of any of the affected employees in relation to whom he envisages taking measures with a view to seeking their agreement to measures to be taken.

(6) In the course of those consultations the employer shall –

> (a) consider any representations made by the appropriate representatives; and

> (b) reply to those representations and, if he rejects any of those representations, state his reasons.

(6A) The employer shall allow the appropriate representatives access to the affected employees and shall afford to those represcntatives such accommodation and other facilities as may be appropriate.

(7) If in any case there are special circumstances which render it not reasonably practicable for an employer to perform a duty imposed on him by any of paragraphs (2) to (6), he shall take all such steps towards performing that duty as are reasonably practicable in the circumstances.

(8) Where –

   (a) the employer has invited any of the affected employees to elect employee representatives, and

   (b) the invitation was issued long enough before the time when the employer is required to give information under paragraph (2) above to allow them to elect representatives by that time, the employer shall be treated as complying with the requirements of this Regulation in relation to those employees if he complies with those requirements as soon as is reasonably practicable after the election of the representatives.

(8A) If, after the employer has invited affected employees to elect representatives, they fail to do so within a reasonable time, he shall give to each affected employee the information set out in paragraph (2).

Regulation 10A

(1) The requirements for the election of employee representatives under Regulation 10(2A) are that –

(a) the employer shall make such arrangements as are reasonably practical to ensure that the election is fair;

(b) the employer shall determine the number of representatives to be elected so that there are sufficient representatives to represent the interests of all the affected employees having regard to the number and classes of those employees;

(c) the employer shall determine whether the affected employees should be represented either by representatives of all the affected employees or by representatives of particular classes of those employees;

(d) before the election the employer shall determine the term of office as employee representatives so that it is of sufficient length to enable information to be given and consultations under Regulation 10 to be completed;

(e) the candidates for election as employee representatives are affected employees on the date of the election;

(f) no affected employee is unreasonably excluded from standing for election;

(g) all affected employees on the date of the election are entitled to vote for employee representatives;

(h)   the employees entitled to vote may vote for as many candidates as there are representatives to be elected to represent them or, if there are to be representatives for particular classes of employees, may vote for as many candidates as there are representatives to be elected to represent their particular class of employee;

(i)   the election is conducted so as to secure that –

   (i)   so far as is reasonably practicable, those voting do so in secret, and

   (ii)   the votes given at the election are accurately counted.

(2)   Where, after an election of employee representatives satisfying the requirements of paragraph (1) has been held, one of those elected ceases to act as an employee representative and any of those employees are no longer represented, those employees shall elect another representative by an election satisfying the requirements of paragraph (1)(a), (e), (f) and (i).

Regulation 11 Failure to inform or consult

(1)   Where an employer has failed to comply with a requirement of Regulation 10 or Regulation 10A, a complaint may be presented to an employment tribunal on that ground –

(a)   in the case of a failure relating to the election of employee representatives, by any of his employees who are affected employees;

(b) in the case of any other failure relating to employee representatives, by any of the employee representatives to whom the failure related,

(c) in the case of failure relating to representatives of a trade union, by the trade union, and

(d) in any other case, by any of his employees who are affected employees.

(2) If on a complaint under paragraph (1) above a question arises whether or not it was reasonably practicable for an employer to perform a particular duty or what steps he took towards performing it, it shall be for him to show –

(a) that there were special circumstances which rendered it not reasonably practicable for him to perform the duty; and

(b) that he took all such steps towards its performance as were reasonably practicable in those circumstances.

[(2A) If on a complaint under paragraph (1) a question arises as to whether or not any employee representative was an appropriate representative for the purposes of Regulation 10, it shall be for the employer to show that the employee representative had the necessary authority to represent the affected employees.

[(2B) On a complaint under sub-paragraph (1)(a) it shall be for the employer to show that the requirements in Regulation 10A have been satisfied.]

(3)   On any such complaint against a transferor that he had failed to perform the duty imposed upon him by virtue of paragraph (2)(d) or, so far as relating thereto, paragraph (7) of Regulation 10 above, he may not show that it was not reasonably practicable for him to perform the duty in question for the reason that the transferee had failed to give him the requisite information at the requisite time in accordance with Regulation 10(3) above unless he gives the transferee notice of his intention to show that fact; and the giving of the notice shall make the transferee a party to the proceedings.

(4)   Where the tribunal finds a complaint under paragraph (1) above well-founded it shall make a declaration to that effect and may –

        (a)   order the employer to pay appropriate compensation to such descriptions of affected employees as may be specified in the award; or

        (b)   if the complaint is that the transferor did not perform the duty mentioned in paragraph (3) above and the transferor (after giving due notice) shows the facts so mentioned, order the transferee to pay appropriate compensation to such descriptions of affected employees as may be specified in the award.

(5)   An employee may present a complaint to an employment tribunal on the ground that he is an employee of a description to which an order under paragraph (4) above relates and that

the transferor or the transferee has failed, wholly or in part, to pay him compensation in pursuance of the order.

(6)   Where the tribunal finds a complaint under paragraph (5) above well-founded it shall order the employer to pay the complainant the amount of compensation which it finds is due to him.

(8)   An employment tribunal shall not consider a complaint under paragraph (1) or (5) above unless it is presented to the tribunal before the end of the period of three months beginning with –

(a)   the date on which the relevant transfer is completed, in the case of a complaint under paragraph (1);

(b)   the date of the tribunal's order under paragraph (4) above, in the case of a complaint under paragraph (5);

or within such further period as the tribunal considers reasonable in a case where it is satisfied that it was not reasonably practicable for the complaint to be presented before the end of the period of three months.

(9)   Section 129 of the 1978 Act (complaint to be sole remedy for breach of relevant rights) and section 133 of that Act (functions of conciliation officer) and Articles 58(2) and 62 of the 1976 Order (which make corresponding provision for Northern Ireland) shall apply to the rights conferred by this Regulation and to proceedings under this Regulation as they

apply to the rights conferred by that Act or that Order and the industrial tribunal proceedings mentioned therein.

(10) An appeal shall lie and shall lie only to the Employment Appeal Tribunal on a question of law arising from any decision of, or arising in any proceedings before, an industrial tribunal under or by virtue of these Regulations; and section 13(1) of the Tribunals and Inquiries Act 1971 (appeal from certain tribunals to the High Court) shall not apply in relation to any such proceedings.

(11) In this Regulation 'appropriate compensation' means such sum not exceeding thirteen weeks' pay for the employee in question as the tribunal considers just and equitable having regard to the seriousness of the failure of the employer to comply with his duty.

(12) Schedule 14 to the 1978 Act or, in Northern Ireland, Schedule 2 to the 1976 Order shall apply for calculating the amount of a week's pay for any employee for the purposes of paragraph (11) above; and, for the purposes of that calculation, the calculation date shall be –

(a) in the case of an employee who is dismissed by reason of redundancy (within the meaning of section 81 of the 1978 Act or, in Northern Ireland, section 11 of the Contracts of Employment and Redundancy Payments Act (Northern Ireland) 1965) the date which is the calculation date for the purposes of any entitlement of his to a redundancy payment (within the meaning of that section) or which would be that calculation date if he were so entitled;

(b)   in the case of an employee who is dismissed for any other reason, the effective date of termination (within the meaning of section 55 of the 1978 Act or, in Northern Ireland, Article 21 of the 1976 Order) of his contract of employment;

(c)   in any other case, the date of the transfer in question.

Regulation 11A Construction of references to employee representatives

For the purposes of Regulations 10 and 11 above persons are employee representatives if –

(a)   they have been elected by employees for the specific purpose of being given information and consulted by their employer under Regulation 10 above; or

(b)   having been elected [or appointed] by employees otherwise than for that specific purpose, it is appropriate (having regard to the purposes for which they were elected) for their employer to inform and consult them under that Regulation,

and (in either case) they are employed by the employer at the time when they are elected or appointed.

Regulation 12 Restriction on contracting out

Any provision of any agreement (whether a contract of employment or not) shall be void in so far as it purports to exclude or limit the operation of Regulation 5, 8 or 10 above or to preclude any person from presenting a complaint to an [employment tribunal] under Regulation 11 above.

Regulation 13 Exclusion of employment abroad or as dock worker

(1)   Regulations 8, 10 and 11 of these Regulations do not apply to employment where under his contract of employment the employee ordinarily works outside the United Kingdom.

(2)   For the purposes of this Regulation a person employed to work on board a ship registered in the United Kingdom shall, unless –

(a)   the employment is wholly outside the United Kingdom, or

(b)   he is not ordinarily resident in the United Kingdom,

be regarded as a person who under his contract ordinarily works in the United Kingdom.

(3)   Nothing in these Regulations applies in relation to any person employed as a registered dock worker unless he is wholly or mainly engaged in work which is not dock work.

(4) Paragraph (3) above shall be construed as if it were contained in section 145 of the 1978 Act.

Regulation 14 Consequential amendments

(1) In section 4(4) of the 1978 Act (written statement to be given to employee on change of his employer), in paragraph (b), the reference to paragraph 17 of Schedule 13 to that Act (continuity of employment where change of employer) shall include a reference to these Regulations.

(2) In section 4(6A) of the Contracts of Employment and Redundancy Payments Act (Northern Ireland) 1965, in paragraph (b), the reference to paragraph 10 of Schedule 1 to that Act shall include a reference to these Regulations.

Signed by order of the Secretary of State.
David Waddington,
Joint Parliamentary Under Secretary of State,
Department of Employment.
14th December 1981.

APPENDIX 3

Acquired Rights Directive 98/50 (Amended Directive)

COUNCIL DIRECTIVE 98/50/EC of 29 June 1998 amending Directive 77/187/EEC on the approximation of the laws of the Member States relating to the safeguarding of employees' rights in the event of transfers of undertakings, businesses or parts of businesses

THE COUNCIL OF THE EUROPEAN UNION,

Having regard to the Treaty establishing the European Community, and in particular Article 100 thereof,

Having regard to the proposal from the Commission (1),

Having regard to the opinion of the European Parliament (2),

Having regard to the opinion of the Economic and Social Committee (3),

Having regard to the opinion of the Committee of the Regions (4),

(1)   Whereas the Community Charter of the fundamental social rights of workers adopted on 9 December 1989 ('Social Charter') states, in points 7, 17 and 18 in particular, that: 'The completion of the internal market must lead to an improvement in the living and working conditions of workers in the European Community. The improvement must cover, where necessary, the development of certain aspects of employment regulations such as procedures for collective redundancies and those regarding bankruptcies. Information, consultation and participation for workers must be developed along appropriate lines, taking account of the practices in force in the various Member States. Such information, consultation and participation must be implemented in due time, particularly in connection with restructuring operations in undertakings or in cases of mergers having an impact on the employment of workers';

(2)   Whereas Directive 77/187/EEC (5) promotes the harmonisation of the relevant national laws ensuring the safeguarding of the rights of employees and requiring transferors and transferees to inform and consult employees' representatives in good time;

(3)   Whereas the purpose of this Directive is to amend Directive 77/187/EEC in the light of the impact of the internal market, the legislative tendencies of the Member States with regard to the rescue of undertakings in economic difficulties, the case-law of the Court of Justice of the European Communities. Council Directive 75/129/EEC of 17 February 1975 on the

approximation of the laws of the Member States relating to collective redundancies (6) and the legislation already in force in most Member States;

(4)   Whereas considerations of legal security and transparency require that the legal concept of transfer be clarified in the light of the case-law of the Court of Justice; whereas such clarification does not alter the scope of Directive 77/187/EEC as interpreted by the Court of Justice;

(5)   Whereas those considerations also require an express provision, in the light of the case-law of the Court of Justice, that Directive 77/187/EEC should apply to private and public undertakings carrying out economic activities, whether or not they operate for gain;

(6)   Whereas it is necessary to clarify the concept of 'employee' in the light of the case-law of the Court of Justice;

(7)   Whereas, with a view to ensuring the survival of insolvent undertakings, Member States should be expressly allowed not to apply Articles 3 and 4 of Directive 77/187/EEC to transfers effected in the framework of liquidation proceedings, and certain derogations from that Directive's general provisions should be permitted in the case of transfers effected in the context of insolvency proceedings;

(8)   Whereas such derogations should also be allowed for one Member State which has special procedures to promote the survival of companies declared to be in a state of economic crisis;

(9)   Whereas the circumstances in which the function and status of employee representatives are to be preserved should be clarified;

(10) Whereas, in order to ensure equal treatment for similar situations, it is necessary to ensure that the information and consultation requirements laid down in Directive 77/187/EEC are complied with irrespective of whether the decision leading to the transfer is taken by the employer or by an undertaking controlling the employer;

(11) Whereas it is appropriate to clarify that, when Member States adopt measures to ensure that the transferee is informed of all the rights and obligations to be transferred, failure to provide that information is not to affect the transfer of the rights and obligations concerned;

(12) Whereas it is necessary to clarify the circumstances in which employees must be informed where there are no employee representatives;

(13) Whereas the Social Charter recognises the importance of the fight against all forms of discrimination, especially based on sex, colour, race, opinion and creed,

HAS ADOPTED THIS DIRECTIVE:

Article 1

Directive 77/187/EEC is hereby amended as follows:

1.   The title shall be replaced by the following: 'Council Directive 77/187/EEC of 14 February 1977 on the approximation of

the laws of the Member States relating to the safeguarding of employees' rights in the event of transfers of undertakings, businesses or parts of undertakings or businesses';

2. Articles 1 to 7 shall be replaced by the following:

Section I Scope and definitions

Article 1

1. (a) This Directive shall apply to any transfer of an undertaking, business, or part of an undertaking or business to another employer as a result of a legal transfer or merger.

    (b) Subject to subparagraph (a) and the following provisions of this Article, there is a transfer within the meaning of this Directive where there is a transfer of an economic entity which retains its identity, meaning an organised grouping of resources which has the objective of pursuing an economic activity, whether or not that activity is central or ancillary.

    (c) This Directive shall apply to public and private undertakings engaged in economic activities whether or not they are operating for gain. An administrative reorganisation of public administrative authorities, or the transfer of administrative functions between public administrative authorities, is not a transfer within the meaning of this Directive.

2.   This Directive shall apply where and in so far as the undertaking, business or part of the undertaking or business to be transferred is situated within the territorial scope of the Treaty.

3.   This Directive shall not apply to sea-going vessels.

Article 2

1.   For the purposes of this Directive:

   (a)   'transferor' shall mean any natural or legal person who, by reason of a transfer within the meaning of Article 1(1), ceases to be the employer in respect of the undertaking, business or part of the undertaking or business;

   (b)   'transferee' shall mean any natural or legal person who, by reason of a transfer within the meaning of Article 1(1), becomes the employer in respect of the undertaking, business or part of the undertaking or business;

   (c)   'representatives of employees' and related expressions shall mean the representatives of the employees provided for by the laws or practices of the Member States;

   (d)   'employee' shall mean any person who, in the Member State concerned, is protected as an employee under national employment law.

2.   This Directive shall be without prejudice to national law as regards the definition of contract of employment or employment relationship. However, Member States shall not

exclude from the scope of this Directive contracts of employment or employment relationships solely because:

(a) of the number of working hours performed or to be performed,

(b) they are employment relationships governed by a fixed-duration contract of employment within the meaning of Article 1(1) of Council Directive 91/383/EEC of 25 June 1991 supplementing the measures to encourage improvements in the safety and health at work of workers with a fixed-duration employment relationship or a temporary employment relationship,* or

(c) they are temporary employment relationships within the meaning of Article 1(2) of Directive 91/383/EEC, and the undertaking, business or part of the undertaking or business transferred is, or is part of, the temporary employment business which is the employer.

Section II Safeguarding of employees' rights

Article 3

1. The transferor's rights and obligations arising from a contract of employment or from an employment relationship existing on the date of a transfer shall, by reason of such transfer, be

---

* *OJ* L206, 29.7.1991, p. 19.

transferred to the transferee. Member States may provide that, after the date of transfer, the transferor and the transferee shall be jointly and severally liable in respect of obligations which arose before the date of transfer from a contract of employment or an employment relationship existing on the date of the transfer.

2.   Member States may adopt appropriate measures to ensure that the transferor notifies the transferee of all the rights and obligations which will be transferred to the transferee under this Article, so far as those rights and obligations are or ought to have been known to the transferor at the time of the transfer. A failure by the transferor to notify the transferee of any such right or obligation shall not affect the transfer of that right or obligation and the rights of any employees against the transferee and/or transferor in respect of that right or obligation.

3.   Following the transfer, the transferee shall continue to observe the terms and conditions agreed in any collective agreement on the same terms applicable to the transferor under that agreement, until the date of termination or expiry of the collective agreement or the entry into force or application of another collective agreement. Member States may limit the period for observing such terms and conditions with the proviso that it shall not be less than one year.

4.   (a)   Unless Member States provide otherwise, paragraphs 1 and 3 shall not apply in relation to employees' rights to old-age, invalidity or survivors' benefits under

supplementary company or inter-company pension schemes outside the statutory social security schemes in Member States.

(b)   Even where they do not provide in accordance with subparagraph (a) that paragraphs 1 and 3 apply in relation to such rights, Member States shall adopt the measures necessary to protect the interests of employees and of persons no longer employed in the transferor's business at the time of the transfer in respect of rights conferring on them immediate or prospective entitlement to old age benefits, including survivors' benefits, under supplementary schemes referred to in subparagraph (a).

Article 4

1.   The transfer of the undertaking, business or part of the undertaking or business shall not in itself constitute grounds for dismissal by the transferor or the transferee. This provision shall not stand in the way of dismissals that may take place for economic, technical or organisational reasons entailing changes in the workforce. Member States may provide that the first subparagraph shall not apply to certain specific categories of employees who are not covered by the laws or practice of the Member States in respect of protection against dismissal.

2.   If the contract of employment or the employment relationship is terminated because the transfer involves a substantial change

in working conditions to the detriment of the employee, the employer shall be regarded as having been responsible for termination of the contract of employment or of the employment relationship.

Article 4a

1. Unless Member States provide otherwise, Articles 3 and 4 shall not apply to any transfer of an undertaking, business or part of an undertaking or business where the transferor is the subject of bankruptcy proceedings or any analogous insolvency proceedings which have been instituted with a view to the liquidation of the assets of the transferor and are under the supervision of a competent public authority (which may be an insolvency practitioner authorised by a competent public authority).

2. Where Articles 3 and 4 apply to a transfer during insolvency proceedings which have been opened in relation to a transferor (whether or not those proceedings have been instituted with a view to the liquidation of the assets of the transferor) and provided that such proceedings are under the supervision of a competent public authority (which may be an insolvency practitioner determined by national law) a Member State may provide that:

    (a) notwithstanding Article 3(1), the transferor's debts arising from any contracts of employment or employment relationships and payable before the transfer or before the opening of the insolvency proceedings shall not be transferred to the transferee, provided that such proceedings give rise, under the law of that Member State, to protection at least equivalent to that provided for in situations covered by Council Directive 80/987/EEC of 20 October 1980 on the approximation of the laws of the Member States relating to the protection of employees in the event of the insolvency of their employer;**

and, or alternatively, that

(b)   the transferee, transferor, or person or persons exercising the transferor's functions, on the one hand, and the representatives of the employees on the other hand may agree alterations, in so far as current law or practice permits, to the employees' terms and conditions of employment designed to safeguard employment opportunities by ensuring the survival of the undertaking, business or part of the undertaking or business.

3.   A Member State may apply paragraph 2(b) to any transfers where the transferor is in a situation of serious economic crisis, as defined by national law, provided that the situation is declared by a competent public authority and open to judicial supervision, on condition that such provisions already exist in national law by 17 July 1998. The Commission shall present a

---

** *OJ* L283, 20.10.1980, p. 23. Directive as amended by Directive 87/164/EEC (*OJ* L66, 11.3.1987, p. 11).

report on the effects of this provision before 17 July 2003 and shall submit any appropriate proposals to the Council.

4.   Member States shall take appropriate measures with a view to preventing misuse of insolvency proceedings in such a way as to deprive employees of the rights provided for in this Directive.

Article 5

1.   If the undertaking, business or part of an undertaking or business preserves its autonomy, the status and function of the representatives or of the representation of the employees affected by the transfer shall be preserved on the same terms and subject to the same conditions as existed before the date of the transfer by virtue of law, regulation, administrative provision or agreement, provided that the conditions necessary for the constitution of the employees' representation are fulfilled. The first subparagraph shall not apply if, under the laws, regulations, administrative provisions or practice in the Member States, or by agreement with the representatives of the employees, the conditions necessary for the reappointment of the representatives of the employees or for the reconstitution of the representation of the employees are fulfilled. Where the transferor is the subject of bankruptcy proceedings or any analogous insolvency proceedings which have been instituted with a view to the liquidation of the assets of the transferor and are under the supervision of a

competent public authority (which may be an insolvency practitioner authorised by a competent public authority), Member States may take the necessary measures to ensure that the transferred employees are properly represented until the new election or designation of representatives of the employees. If the undertaking, business or part of an undertaking or business does not preserve its autonomy, the Member States shall take the necessary measures to ensure that the employees transferred who were represented before the transfer continue to be properly represented during the period necessary for the reconstitution or reappointment of the representation of employees in accordance with national law or practice.

2. If the term of office of the representatives of the employees affected by the transfer expires as a result of the transfer, the representatives shall continue to enjoy the protection provided by the laws, regulations, administrative provisions or practice of the Member States.

Section III Information and consultation

Article 6

1. The transferor and transferee shall be required to inform the representatives of their respective employees affected by the transfer of the following:

     —   the date or proposed date of the transfer,

–   the reasons for the transfer,

–   the legal, economic and social implications of the transfer for the employees,

–   any measures envisaged in relation to the employees.

The transferor must give such information to the representatives of his employees in good time before the transfer is carried out.

The transferee must give such information to the representatives of his employees in good time, and in any event before his employees are directly affected by the transfer as regards their conditions of work and employment.

2.   Where the transferor or the transferee envisages measures in relation to his employees, he shall consult the representatives of his employees in good time on such measures with a view to reaching an agreement.

3.   Member States whose laws, regulations or administrative provisions provide that representatives of the employees may have recourse to an arbitration board to obtain a decision on the measures to be taken in relation to employees may limit the obligations laid down in paragraphs 1 and 2 to cases where the transfer carried out gives rise to a change in the business likely to entail serious disadvantages for a considerable number of the employees. The information and consultations shall cover at least the measures envisaged in relation to the employees. The information must be provided and

consultations taken place in good time before the change in the business as referred to in the first subparagraph is effected.

4.   The obligations laid down in this Article shall apply irrespective of whether the decision resulting in the transfer is taken by the employer or an undertaking controlling the employer. In considering alleged breaches of the information and consultation requirements laid down by this Directive, the argument that such a breach occurred because the information was not provided by an undertaking controlling the employer shall not be accepted as an excuse.

5.   Member States may limit the obligations laid down in paragraphs 1, 2 and 3 to undertakings or businesses which, in terms of the number of employees, meet the conditions for the election or nomination of a collegiate body representing the employees.

6.   Member States shall provide that, where there are no representatives of the employees in an undertaking or business through no fault of their own, the employees concerned must be informed in advance of:

–   the date or proposed date of the transfer,

–   the reason for the transfer,

–   the legal, economic and social implications of the transfer for the employees,

–   any measures envisaged in relation to the employees.

Section IV Final provisions

Article 7

This Directive shall not affect the right of Member States to apply or introduce laws, regulations or administrative provisions which are more favourable to employees or to promote or permit collective agreements or agreements between social partners more favourable to employees.

Article 7a

Member States shall introduce into their national legal systems such measures as are necessary to enable all employees and representatives of employees who consider themselves wronged by failure to comply with the obligations arising from this Directive to pursue their claims by judicial process after possible recourse to other competent authorities.

Article 7b

The Commission shall submit to the Council an analysis of the effects of the provisions of this Directive before 17 July 2006. It shall propose any amendment which may seem necessary.

Article 2

1. Member States shall bring into force the laws, regulations and administrative provisions necessary to comply with this

Directive by 17 July 2001 at the latest or shall ensure that, by that date, at the latest, the employers' and employees' representatives have introduced the required provisions by means of agreement, Member States being obliged to take the necessary steps enabling them at all times to guarantee the results imposed by this Directive.

2.   When Member States adopt the measures referred to in paragraph 1, they shall contain a reference to this Directive or shall be accompanied by such reference on the occasion on their official publication. The methods of making such reference shall be laid down by Member States. Member States shall inform the Commission immediately of the measures they take to implement this Directive.

Article 3

This Directive shall enter into force on the day of its publication in the *Official Journal of the European Communities*.

Article 4

This Directive is addressed to the Member States.

Done at Luxembourg, 29 June 1998.
For the Council
The President
R. COOK

Further reading

Below are some texts which you will find very useful to follow up points/queries:

- Bourn et al. (1999) *The Transfer of Undertakings in the Public Sector.* Dartmouth: Aldershot (very useful for contracting out issues).

- Cavalier (1997) *Transfer Rights: TUPE in Perspective.* London: Institute of Employment Rights (very useful overview).

- Hardy (2001) 'The Acquired Rights Directive: A Case of Economic and Social Rights at Work', in Collins, Davies and Rideout (eds), *Legal Regulation of the Employment Relation.* Netherlands: Kluwer, Chapter 24.

- Hardy and Adnett (1999) 'Entrepreneurial Freedom versus Employee Rights: the Acquired Rights Directive and EU Social Policy post-Amsterdam', *Journal of European Social Policy.*

- Hardy and Painter (1999) 'The New Acquired Rights Directive and Its Implications for European Employee Relations in the Twenty-First Century', *Maastricht Journal of European and Comparative Law.*

- Harvey (2000) *Harvey on Industrial Relations and Employment Law* (Division F). London: Butterworths (the practising employment lawyer's text).

- Lee Cooke et al. (2000) *For Better and for Worse? Transfer of Undertakings and the Reshaping of Employment Relations*, Working Paper 13, The Future of Work Project, EWERC/ESRC, UMIST (very recent and interesting empirical research report on changes post-transfer and other perceptions of the law and TUPE).

- McMullen (2000) *Business Transfers and Employee Rights*. London: Butterworths (a comprehensive loose-leaf file written by the UK's leading expert).

- Napier (1993) *CCT, Market Testing and Employment Rights: The Effects of TUPE and the Acquired Rights Directive*. London: Institute of Employment Rights (good discussion of CCT and TUPE).

- Sparke (1996) *The CCT Guide*. London: Butterworths (very useful on CCT and TUPE).

- Staffordshire University Press, Stoke-on-Trent, research report presenting views on TUPE.

Useful websites

For DTI Consultation on TUPE see:

www.dti.gov.uk

For 'Staff Transfers in the Public Sector: Statement of Practice', January 2000 see:

www.cabinet.office.gov.uk/
civilservice/2000/tupe

Other useful websites:

ACAS: www.acas.org.uk

CBI: www.cbi.org.uk

CCTA Government Information Service:

www.open.gov.uk/index.html

Context: case law on CD-Rom with on-line updates:

www.justis.com

CORDIS research database: www.cordis.lu

Croner's English and EU case law on line:

www.newlawonline.com

Department of Trade and Industry:

www.dti.gov.uk

Employment Appeals Tribunal: www.employmentappeals.gov.uk

Employment Law on a Disc: www.emplaw.co.uk

EU agencies and bodies: Europa.eu.int/en/agencies.html

EU Commission: Europa.eu.int/en/comm.html

EU Commission: Official Documents:

Europa.eu.int/comm/
off/en/index.htm

EU Employers' Network: www.euen.co.uk

EU Glossary: www.abdn.ac.uk/~po1028/
                           sources/europe.htm

EU recent developments: Europa.eu.int/geninfo/
                           whatsnew.htm

European Court of Justice: Curia.eu.int/en/index.htm

European Industrial Relations Observatory:

www.eiro.eurofound.ie

European Trade Union Confederation:

www.etuc.org

HMSO – government Stationery Office (e.g. for Bills):

www.parliament.the-stationery-
office.co.uk

HM Treasury: www.hm-treasury.gov.uk/
                           main_index95.html

Incomes Data Services: www.incomesdata.co.uk

Institute of Personnel and Development (CIPD):

www.cipd.co.uk

Judicial Business of the House of Lords:

      www.parliament.the-stationery-
office.co.uk/pa/ld/ldjudinf.htm

Labour Research Department: www.lrd.org.uk

Law Commission: www.gtnet.gov.uk/klawcomm/
homepage.htm

Law Professors' Network: www.law.cam.ac.uk/jurist/
jur-uk.htm

Law Rights: free legal information for England and Wales:

      www.lawrights.co.uk

Society for Human Resources Management:

      www.shrm.org

Tolley on-line: www.tolley.co.uk

TUC: www.tuc.org.uk

UK Central Government: a central index for government
departments on the Web: www.open.gov.uk/cctagis/
central.htm

UK Department of Education and Employment:

      www.open.gov.uk/dfee/
dfeehome.htm

UK Government Information Service:

      www.gtnet.gov.uk

UK Law on-line: www.leeds.ac.uk/law/hamlyn

UK Legal: www.uklegal.com

UK Parliament: www.parliament.the-stationery-
                             office.co.uk

See Bibliography for fuller list of references.

Bibliography

Adnett, N. (1996) *Compulsory Competitive Tendering and the Acquired Rights Directive: Winner's Curse and the ETO Defence*, Division of Economics Working Paper No. 96.5, May 1996, Staffordshire University, UK.

Audit Commission (1987) *Competitiveness and Contracting Out of Local Authorities*. HMSO.

Audit Commission (1989) *Preparing for Compulsory Competition*, Occasional Paper. HMSO.

Audit Commission (1994) *Realising the Benefit of Competition – The Client Role for Contracted Services*. HMSO.

Audit Commission (1995) *Making Markets: A Review of the Audits of the Client Role for Contracted Services*. HMSO.

Barnard, C. (2000) *EC Employment Law*, 2nd edn. Wiley.

Bishop, M. and Kay, J. (eds) (1993) *European Mergers and Merger Policy*. Oxford University Press.

Blank, R. (ed.) (1994) *Social Protection versus Economic Flexibility*. University of Chicago Press.

Bowers, D. and Elias, P. (1996) *Transfers of Undertakings*, 4th edn. Longman.

Cirell, S. and Bennett, J. (1990) *CCT Law and Practice*. Longman.

Davies, P. (1989) 'Acquired rights, creditors rights, freedom of contract and industrial democracy', *Yearbook of European Law*. Kluwer.

Davies, P. and Freedland, M. (1982) *Transfer of Employment*. Oxford.

Deakin, S. and Morris, G. (1999) *Labour Law*, 2nd edn. Butterworths.

Department of Employment (n.d.) *Employment Rights on the Transfer of an Undertaking*, Public Information Booklet PL 699 (revised version). HMSO.

Department of Employment (1984) Press Notice, 15 November. HMSO.

DE (1986) *Building Businesses not Barriers*, Cmnd. 9794. HMSO.

DE (1988) *Employment for the 1990s*, Cmnd. 540. HMSO.

Elias, P. and Bowers, D. (1985) *Pitfalls of Transfers of Undertakings*. Longman.

EOC Report (1995) *The Gender Impact of CCT in Local Government*, Research Discussion Series No. 12. EOC.

EU Parliament (1993) *Record of the EP Plenary Session, 13–16 December, 1993*. Strasbourg.

EU Commission (1976) *Report of the Committee of Experts on the ARD*. Luxembourg.

EU Commission (1989) *Social Action Plan*, COM (89) 568. Luxembourg.

EU Commission (1990) *XXth Report on Competition Policy*. Luxembourg.

Flynn, N. and Strehl, F. (1993) *Public Sector Management in Europe*. Prentice Hall.

Hansard – HC (1981):

   10 March, col. 756;

   7 December, cols. 684–79;

   17 December, col. 680.

   HMSO.

Hansard – HC (1993):

   21 January, cols. 505–10.

   HMSO.

Hansard – HC (1996):

   6 February, cols. 197–208.

   HMSO.

Hansard – HL (1981):

   10 December, col. 1490.

   HMSO.

Hansard – HL (1986):

   17 July, col. 1057;

   24 July, col. 450.

   HMSO.

Hansard – HL (1987):

   25 March, cols. 260–82;

   9 December, col. 427.

   HMSO.

Hansard – HL (1996):

   4 June, cols. 1191–206.

   HMSO.

Hardy, S. (1995) 'Acquiring revised rights: TUPE Regulations and recent developments', in Slapper, G. (ed.), *Companies in the 1990s*, Chapter 7. Cavendish.

Harvey et al. (1997) *Harvey on Industrial Relations and Employment Law*. Butterworths.

HM Government (1992) *Market Testing Guidance*. HMSO.

HM Government (1993) *Guidance to Market Testing*. HMSO.

House of Lords (1996) *Transfer of Undertakings: Acquired Rights*, 5th Report, Session 1995–96, House of Lords Select Committee on the EC, HL Paper 38. HMSO.

Kerr, A. and Radford, M. (1995) 'CCT Challenged', *New Economy*, vol. 2, Spring, p. 36.

Local Government Chronicle (1995) 17 November.

Local Government Information Unit (1993) *CCT: On the Record – A Review of the Experiences of CCT under the Local Government Act 1988*. LGIU.

Local Government Management Board (1994) *CCT Information Service Survey, 10 December 1994*. LGMB.

Local Government Management Board (1995) *LMGB Survey, September 1995*. LGMB.

McMullen, J. (1991) *Business Transfers and Employee Rights*, 2nd edn. Butterworths.

McMullen, J. (1994) 'Contracting-out and market testing – the uncertainty ends?', *Industrial Law Journal*, vol. 23, no. 3, September, pp. 230–41.

McMullen, J. (1996) 'Atypical transfers, atypical workers and atypical employment structures – a case for greater transparency in the transfer of employment issues', *Industrial Law Journal*, vol. 25, no. 4, December, pp. 286–95.

More, G. (1995) 'The Acquired Rights Directive: frustrating or facilitating labour market flexibility?', in J. Shaw and G. More (eds), *New Legal Dynamics of European Union*, Chapter 8. Oxford University Press.

Municipal Journal (1994) 22 December.

Napier, B. (1993) *CCT, Market Testing and Employment Rights: The Effects of TUPE and the Acquired Rights Directive*, May 1993. Institute of Employment Rights.

Napier, B. (1994) 'Using Community law to protect workers' rights: a case study', in P. O'Higgins, K. Ewing, C. Gearty and B. Hepple (eds), *Human Rights and Labour Law*. Mansell.

NATFHE (1994) *Prison Education After Competitive Tendering*. Natfhe Surveys.

Ogus, A. (1994) *Regulation*. Oxford University Press.

O'Halloran, M. (1993) 'Acquired rights and TUPE … What's going on?', *Journal of the Association of Metropolitan Authorities*, September, p. 12.

Office of Public Services (1993) *Government Guidance on TUPE: 11 March 1993*, OPSS 30/93. HMSO.

Rao, N. and Young, K. (1995) *Competition, Contracts and Change – The Local Authority Experience of CCT*, LGC & Joseph Rowntree Foundation Study.

Shanks, M. (1977) 'The social policy of the EC', *Common Market Law Review*, vol. 14, pp. 373–80.

Shaw, J. and More, G. (eds) (1995) *New Legal Dynamics of European Union*. Oxford University Press.

Sparke, A. (1996) *The CCT Guide*, 2nd edn. Butterworths.

Szymanski, S. (1993) 'Cheap rubbish? Competitive tendering and contracting out in refuse collection: 1981–88', *Journal of Fiscal Studies*, vol. 14, pp. 109–30.

Szymanski, S. (1993) *A Statistical Analysis of CCT in Refuse Collection*. CDC Publishing.

Szymanski, S. (1994) *DSOs and Private Contractors*. CDC Publishing.

Szymanski, S. (1994) 'CCT: a clean solution?', *New Economy*, vol. 1, Summer, p. 89.

Vincent-Jones, P. (1994) 'The limits of contractual order in public sector transacting', *Legal Studies* (Journal of the SPTL), vol. 14, no. 3, November, pp. 364–92.

Walsh, K. and Davis, H. (1993) *The Impact of the Local Government Act 1988*. HMSO.

Wilson, J. (1994) 'Competitive tendering and UK public services', *Economic Review*, April, p. 34.

Younson, F. (1989) *Employment Law and Business Transfers: A Practical Guide*. Butterworths.